THRIVING IN INTERSECTIONALITY

THRIVING IN INTERSECTIONALITY

IMMIGRANTS, BELONGING, AND CORPORATE AMERICA

Karen,
Keep thriving!
Lola A.
2022

LOLA M. ADEYEMO

NEW DEGREE PRESS

THRIVING IN INTERSECTIONALITY
Immigrants, Belonging, and Corporate America

ISBN   979-8-88504-578-0   *Paperback*
           979-8-88504-923-8   *Kindle Ebook*
           979-8-88504-694-7   *Ebook*

This book is for you, Daddy and Mummy.

Prof. Joseph Kayode Ogunmoyela (1951–2015)

and

Mrs. Patricia Adebola Ogunmoyela (1953–2015)

I miss you both.

But I am forever grateful I get to be called your daughter.

Thank you for building the foundation of my identity and belonging story and for setting me on the path to my future.

CONTENTS

———

INTRODUCTION

In the spring of 2012 in San Diego, California, I attended an all-day workshop with a cross-functional project team at work. During the session break, a white older guy next to me asked where I was from originally. After I responded, "Nigeria," he asked if my family was still there. When I replied yes, he continued by asking, "Are they trying to come over?" I was confused and asked what he meant. He said, "Well, are you able to bring them over?"

When it finally dawned on me what his question meant, my first reaction was anger. Why did he automatically assume that my family was trying to "escape" my home country to come into the USA? My second reaction was that of embarrassment because people in the room had heard his statements and assumption.

After thinking about it, I realized he didn't mean to be insulting, so I decided not to be rude in return. I replied, "No, they are not trying to move here. They don't want to immigrate." I could tell he was very surprised and a little confused. This conversation was one of many such conversations that I had at work, and it continuously highlighted the different assumptions some people make about immigrants in the United States, even in the workplace.

I was born and raised in Nigeria, West Africa, where I spent the first twenty-five years of my life. Culturally in Nigeria, women experience less career pressure than men and generally not as much expectation to pursue an advanced degree and a professional career path. Fortunately for me, I was raised to go after what I wanted and had a few female role models in my family as well. After getting my bachelor's degree, I immediately started applying for graduate schools outside of Nigeria. I always knew I wanted to explore what other career paths and opportunities were available. After two years of work experience, I got accepted into a program I wanted and quit my corporate job with a global brand to immigrate to the United States. When I moved to the United States for graduate school, this would be my first time living outside of Nigeria, and I became an immigrant.

Coming to the United States and into the corporate workforce, I faced the continued barriers as a woman, which I expected. However, in addition to the difficulties I faced as a woman in corporate America, I realized I am also a Black woman in America. And I had to deal with people's perceptions of immigrants.

The words "immigrant" and "Black" have taken on new meanings for me as a corporate employee in America. The experience I described above occurred at work, one of many. It made me wonder, *What other assumptions have been formed about my identity in the workplace?*

THE STATE OF CORPORATE AMERICA AND THE DIVERSITY, INCLUSION EFFORTS

In the United States, the word "immigrant" is often associated with undocumented or underprivileged individuals escaping their country or seeking low-wage jobs. Therefore, the discussions around immigration center around documentation and legality of residence. According to the PEW Research Institute analysis of the latest US census survey, a significant percentage of the overall immigrant population is documented. Most documented immigrants are also likely to hold a college degree. As corporate America battles to build inclusive workplaces, the immigrants' perspectives in the workplace become essential to including everyone. How does our cultural identity impact how we are treated at work? Most importantly, how have these cultural backgrounds and identities influenced how we get our jobs done and advance in corporate America?

The misconceptions about immigrants leave out individuals who are well educated and also have strong family or emotional ties to their home country or immigrant communities and cultures and have career advancement goals. As we discuss inclusion within the large corporate workforce, capturing the voices and perspectives of immigrants is an essential aspect of understanding the increasingly multicultural and multigenerational workplace. Building true inclusion in corporate America can benefit from incorporating the perspectives of populations most likely to feel excluded at work—those with more than one underrepresentation dimension.

For the longest time, all I had heard about "immigrants" was that they were people who escaped something. Since my immediate family was in Nigeria and I could visit when I wanted, I didn't always associate the word "immigrant" with myself. I moved to America to go to school, and I stayed for better job opportunities in the corporate space and to start my family. However, I did immigrate and now consider America my home as well. While immigration issues are valid and conversations concerning documentation are still very much needed in America, we also need a focused conversation on the corporate workplace. We need to have specific conversations that supports inclusion for the immigrant population in the workplace.

WHAT IS "INTERSECTIONALITY"?

According to Merriam-Webster, intersectionality is defined as "the complex, cumulative way in which the effects of multiple forms of discrimination (such as racism, sexism, and classism) combine and overlap, particularly in the experiences of marginalized individuals or groups." The word was first introduced in 1989 by civil rights activist and professor Kimberlé Crenshaw, who coined the term to describe the way social identities can overlap. This word, though relatively new, is becoming increasingly important in the diversity, equity, and inclusion conversations in the workplace. It allows for recognizing the cumulative effects of multiple identities, which is different from a single isolated under representation category. In corporate America today, we are broadening the definitions of inclusion to accommodate an intersectional lens. This perspective will ensure that we capture the voices and needs of the employees that need it the most. One category that is not often discussed as a part of this intersectionality conversation is the "immigrant" category.

BEING A WOMAN, A PERSON OF COLOR, AND AN IMMIGRANT

As an immigrant woman in corporate America, functioning at the triple intersection of gender, ethnicity, and immigrant status requires a lot of personal effort to thrive against barriers that exclude immigrants. The experiences from the first twenty-five years of my life are a large part of my identity, beliefs, and value system. I am an American but also primarily Nigerian. Being an immigrant from Nigeria, what has shaped my value system comes from my religious upbringing, how women are raised in my home country, and how I was raised in my home to survive in that environment. In Nigeria, women are expected to be submissive and build a good home. I have been raised to value that while being willing to think outside of the societal boxes and pursue any goals that I want. While women have successful careers, the journey is not an easy one. The values and expectations translate into how we show up at work and interact with the workplace. As we have the conversations around belonging in the American corporate workplace, immigrant women can experience things similarly and struggle with the same hurdles to advance.

Moving to the United States in 2009 as an adult, I have spent most of my life in America as a corporate employee. I spent my first year as a full-time college student and then got my first job in a global corporation. I have since moved through different large-sized, global American companies with thousands of employees. I didn't grow up seeing many women in the corporate world, and I naturally connected primarily with other women at work. I am compelled to write this book because of my personal experiences and the common threads that I have observed in conversations with other immigrant women at work.

This book holds insights from my personal experience as well as the stories and experiences of immigrant women from different countries of origin and at different roles and career stages in corporate America. The stories and examples provide insights into how immigrant women experience similar challenges and leverage their unique intersectional and cultural identities to show up and thrive in corporate America. How do we perceive things differently because of our cultural background? Understanding these nuances can help to lean on our identities, draw out strengths, and guide career decisions. They impact the way of work and can help to promote authenticity and build inclusion. The uniqueness of the immigrant voice and values are vital to understanding the rich corporate employee mix and supporting women and all immigrants to thrive at work.

WHY FOCUS ON "THRIVING" AT THE IMMIGRANT INTERSECTION AT WORK?

According to Merriam-Webster, a definition of "thrive" is "to progress toward or realize a goal despite or because of circumstances."

As someone who moved to the United States coming from a small town with friends and neighbors around me, I didn't grow up feeling like the "other" in my communities. After going through the legal process to get into the United States, I eventually converted from student visa to green card and work authorization holder, and finally to US citizenship. My career has taken me through different roles and within different global organizations in the United States. I currently support corporations as a certified diversity professional focused on building inclusive spaces through employee resource groups (ERG) and inclusive formal work groups. I am one of many thriving despite the multiple exclusion stories, barriers, and culturally different perspectives. Because I can relate, because I constantly see these barriers holding immigrants back in my role, slowing our inclusion efforts, I recognize the gap and the opportunity to do more to eliminate barriers and help more immigrants thrive at work.

This book is a resource for educated, professional immigrant women who want to work or already work in and ultimately seek to thrive in corporate organizations. The stories provide learnings from the experiences of those who have successfully stepped in, tips they have leveraged to overcome challenges, and how they have turned their identity and upbringing to an advantage to thrive in corporate America. This book is also a resource for diversity, equity, and inclusion professionals and leaders seeking to build inclusive workplaces.

The topics this book covers ultimately brings together "immigration in America" and overlays it with "inclusion within the corporate workplace." These topics, conversations, and perspectives are important because sometimes we forget that at the heart of these conversations are people with a desire to thrive at work despite multiple intersections and cultural backgrounds. Understanding the immigrant experience in the workplace through stories accomplishes three main things: directly addressing the stigma, encouraging the participation of immigrants at work, and advancing the structural and policy changes that need to happen to address these intentional or unintentional prejudicial acts against immigrants in the corporate workplaces.

SECTION I

WHO AM I?

"I am just one of millions of people who have been told that in order to fulfill my dreams, in order to contribute my talents to the world, I have to resist the truth of who I am. I, for one, am ready to stop resisting and to start existing as my full and authentic self."

—AMERICA FERRERA

CHAPTER ONE

IDENTITY AT WORK

―――

INTRODUCTION

I am an immigrant. I moved from Nigeria by choice, and I have made the United States of America my home. The word "immigrant" refers to someone who came into a different country to live, as I have done. However, when I think about my children, who were all born here, I don't think of them as immigrants. Why would they be? They were born here and did not move here. This was my belief before I started working on this book. But, as I conducted the research and the interviews for this book, that definition has become a little blurry. In my conversations with other women who identified as immigrants, I have heard a broad spectrum of definition from different people. These range from women who were born in the US but whose family immigrated to the US decades earlier, to women who have been in the United States since they were children, to those who just immigrated to the United States as adults by choice, all identifying strongly as immigrants.

Assimilation—the process of adopting and fitting into the dominant culture—is a natural order when you get started within a new system: a new country, city, neighborhood, church, and organization. When we start a new job, we naturally observe what is being done and blend into the culture— the way things are done, at least at the start. Eventually, as we get comfortable, we strive to introduce our own style, if it is welcome and safe. How strongly is an immigrant identity safe in the workplace? Does choosing to adopt certain behaviors and practices while toning down on our cultural persona make us more "American" and blend in more at work? Maybe. Even if you are born in America, the ties to cultural heritage can vary and determine what authentic behaviors we portray in the workplace. If we truly wanted to go by genealogy, maybe everyone should be labeled as an immigrant because we all came from somewhere. Ultimately, we have our reasons for choosing how to describe ourselves and how much of our culture we hold onto. Once we get into the workplace, we don't ever really get a chance to explain our legal or generation status. What we do bring with us are the behaviors and beliefs that may help or hinder us in the workplace, regardless of how much we try to adapt to the existing organizational culture.

"Assimilation, not success, is the American end game."

—EUNY HONG

WHAT IS IN A NAME?
NAME AND CREDIBILITY

Aline Estefam was born and raised in Brazil and got her bachelor's degree in architecture. Although she had risen to a director level in Sao Paulo, she was frustrated with the bureaucracy and the difficulty in executing projects she was passionate about. Sharing her motivation for moving to the United States during our interview, Aline explains, "I started watching videos like lectures and talks from urban planners and people that I thought were very good in my area, and I realized that almost everyone was from the US." She decided to apply to come to the United States to get a master's degree. Her original plan was to go back after her program and implement what she learned, but she eventually decided to stay and try to find a job.

Bringing her prior experiences as well as her US master's degree, Aline felt she was ready and qualified to do the type of work she wanted. When she started her job search process, the rejection letters piled up. When she followed up with the recruiters, she got feedback that the hiring team didn't get a clear impression that she had the experiences she listed. "In Brazil, we have the tendency of not talking about ourselves, saying we are good about different things because we see it as not polite." She learned it was important to let people know what you could do verbally in addition to the resume.

Another area Aline found a big opportunity to change the narrative about herself in the professional space was in her name pronunciation. Her birth name is spelled "A-L-I-N-E," a common name in Brazil. The first pronunciation that people say is like the train: "A-line." Explaining the pronunciation in English takes some time, and it was not a conversation she always wanted to lead with at work.

"We would start all the meetings with people asking me how to pronounce my name and where was it from? And where was I from? And then we'll talk about my personal life, you know, and why the US, so it will kind of shift the conversation."

As someone in a leadership role, Aline wanted to drive the direction of the conversations from the start and command respect. She saw her name consistently set the tone for the conversation, and she didn't want that. When she began managing a large client project, she wanted to be respected and trusted and decided to change her name to Ali. "I felt if I changed my name, maybe something would happen, and it really did." She wasn't sure if this was because the name sounded masculine or if the fact that it was a more familiar name drew fewer questions, but she stuck with her name as Ali.

Aline Estefam currently serves as the vice president of planning and design of a company in New York, and she describes the frequent struggle she still faces in having to prove her competency, especially managing people who are older and assume she is incompetent because of various reasons, including being an immigrant. She once had a direct hire verbally lash out to her at work and threaten to take company materials because of a work issue. Having someone who reports to her publicly question her authority and criticize her competency was stressful. "He said he didn't think that I knew what I was doing. I wasn't a good manager because I'm not even from the US. How can I come and manage him?" Fortunately for Aline, when she escalated the issue to her leadership team, she was supported. As immigrant women, regardless of the level of experience, relying on the resume, experience level, and qualifications alone to prove capability can be ineffective, and there is a need for additional support from the organization to establish credibility. We will dive more into support in the chapter on representation and mentorship.

NAME AND ACCENT

Different factors shape our identities. Geographical location, our community, the choices our parents made for us, and even the media plays a large part. For Susan Oguche, it was a combination of some of these factors that impacted her early identity. Susan was born in Nigeria and immigrated with her family at age five. She was raised in small cities in the Southern United States and later in Ohio and didn't grow up with a lot of close Black American friends. Susan knew most of the friends she had around were the children of other African immigrants or white Americans.

"I feel that my parents tried to kind of shield us from what they perceived were the negative aspects of the Black experience. They saw so much negativity around being Black in America and they probably had some of their own negative stereotype about Black Americans. I knew other Nigerians or Ghanaians or Cameroonians, but I didn't have many Black American friends."

Susan Oguche noticed in high school that with an English first name and having lost her African accent, people found it difficult to identify her background. However, she also observed that when white people found out about her African heritage, they would sometimes draw comparisons between her and non-African Blacks. "I've had teachers and bosses say, 'You're not like a regular Black person.'" When people made this and similar racist and hurtful statements, it really highlighted to Susan some of the privileges she had that many other people did not get. Getting into the workplace in a communications career, she also began to realize that she had the privilege of masquerading behind her name and her voice. "I have this English name, and then I have this white-sounding voice, and I've had to really be intentional in understanding how that's given me privilege." In the workplace, there are biases and stereotypes against individuals based on accents and names. Having both an English name and a speaking voice that lacked a noticeable foreign accent, people did not immediately realize she was an immigrant. That is a privilege.

As a communications professional, the media also played a large role in the identity she craved and created for herself. Susan Oguche had grown up watching CNN and looking up to CNN reporters, and as a result of her upbringing and professional training, she developed the acquired style of speaking. Although it wasn't a goal she set out to achieve, it was a combined result of her background and upbringing. Early in her career, Susan once had an opportunity to be on national TV for an effort she was leading. Susan's boss passed over the opportunity because they had a noticeable accent, so Susan was the one best positioned to do the feature. "I stepped into this opportunity, and I was able to speak and present in the acceptable professional accent." She went from a childhood of being boldly Nigerian to getting into the workplace and becoming very aware of the emphasis on accents and names.

"I felt like I always had a different work life versus personal life because in my personal life, I'm very much Nigerian. My husband, both my parents, most of my close friends are Nigerians and I felt like I was fully my immigrant self at home. But when I went to work, it just was different."

As immigrants, our background is shaped by different factors, and many immigrants step into the workplace with the feeling of needing to be who the workplace wants us to be. In addition to any visible attribute seen at work, immigrants are stepping into the subjective perspective of coworkers and leaders. No one really knows anyone's story, but people make assumptions about immigrants from certain parts of the world. At work, we try to understand what is acceptable and adopt the behaviors.

For Susan, the duality was sustainable for a while, but as she advanced in her career, the efforts and hours she put in at work grew longer, and the growth was not happening. It took working in a toxic work environment where she really felt unappreciated as a person to begin the journey to finding her own authenticity at work.

"I got to the point where I was really struggling with my mental health, and I just told my husband I'm quitting. And I did. I realized I was being pushed out, but I really needed to take a step back and own my own identity so I could find a place to work that appreciated me for myself."

As working professionals, the largest portion of our waking hours is spent in the workplace. Working in a space that demands a different identity than what is natural for us can be a major challenge and is not sustainable. For Susan Oguche, that stress pushed her out of the workplace, but she was grateful for the much-needed opportunity to reset. Ultimately, she was able to embark on a journey that leveraged external mentors and coaches who encouraged her to step into her authentic identity so she could find the right workplace.

AUTHENTICITY AT WORK
AUTHENTIC VOICE

Our families and community also have a strong impact on our identity growing up. As we evolve, sometimes the identity we create through that process might be different from who we really want to be. If we end up carrying the created identity to work, we will come to a point where we might have to reassess our career choices. For Trish Lindo, growing up and blending in was the easy default, and this translated into the workplace. Trish was born in Jamaica but immigrated with her family to the United States when she was eight years old. She grew up in Hollywood, Florida. Although her stepdad was American, her mother, a very strong presence in her life, had a strong cultural Jamaican presence. Trish grew up eating Jamaican food and learning about the culture from her mother while trying to blend into the American culture. "I see myself as an immigrant and I do understand what it feels like not to be part of something or part of community. I do feel like an 'other.'" This —feeling outside of the majority—is amplified for immigrants in the workplace.

As a young child, Trish saw firsthand how her mother was treated negatively as a Jamaican immigrant. She grew up observing people's negative reactions and assumptions in public places because her mother was not speaking what people termed the proper Queen's English. "It was very important for me to blend in. I had an accent myself and got teased. I learned very quickly as a kid not to draw attention to myself." Growing up in South Florida, albeit multicultural, the perspective Trish had as a child was the pressure to blend in and not stand out. It wasn't until she attended a historically Black university that she realized for the first time that it was okay to be Jamaican. "I met other students who proudly shared where they were from and spoke other languages. I realized I could share my identity and origin as being from Jamaica and that was new for me."

Getting into the workplace, Trish found that it was easy to default to behaviors that drew the least attention to herself at work. Earlier in her career, this was easily achieved. "I was just trying to fit in. In my industry, you start off at the bottom of the ladder. You do whatever it takes, you do what you're told, you don't make waves because you want to keep your job and you need the money." In most of the spaces, people faced repercussions for speaking out at work against the popular majority and for speaking up, sharing perspectives and ideas considered "making waves." "I worked in the entertainment industry for many years and that ability to adapt served me very well. It is implied that you need to blend in. No one says it." However, because of Trish's background experiences, she started being more aware of her unique perspectives, and she wanted to advance inclusivity. Although it was easier to blend in and agree with the majority, she was in a constant struggle to find her voice and speak up.

Trish Lindo's career has taken her across multiple global organizations, and the culture in these spaces varies. She found that she began to consciously move toward roles and spaces where she was encouraged to bring her perspectives. As she moved to a different industry, she took roles where different lenses and different perspectives drive values for her teams. In her current role as creator manager at a large tech company, one of the lessons her mother taught her in childhood guides her work daily: "Treat people well, treat everybody fairly, and stand up for yourself." Trish Lindo currently gets to work with different people from different communities and countries, and her ears are always tuned for creative avenues and inclusive ways to improve results.

Because of how we have lived, how we grew up, and the situations we have encountered, we all have unique identities; even when initially subdued, we evolve to a place where hiding ourselves cannot be sustained. Our upbringing and talents might require stepping outside of our comfort zone as we embark on our career paths, but as we continue the journey, our identities are revealed and leveraged to thrive in our roles.

Belonging is a personal journey; it began where we started.

AUTHENTIC STYLE AND EXPRESSION

Unlike Susan Oguche and Trish Lindo, who were brought into the United States as children, the journey of identity for immigrants who come into the United States as adults can look different. For Sandra Morales, she started her work experience in Bogota, Colombia, where she was born and raised. When she came to the United States, she was already a working professional. She settled in Portland and lived in a community where there were little to no Latina residents.

A major negative experience for her was the pushback to her style and expression. In Colombia, her physical appearance reflected an expressive style. Sandra dressed to look good and enjoyed using makeup to accentuate her appearance. Translating this to her workplace in America, however, she got a lot of feedback about the lack of "professionalism" in her dress code at work. "I got complaints that I dressed in a provocative manner that was inappropriate for a work setting, and I changed my appearance and expression different times to try to copy what I see in America. It was very overwhelming and emotionally taxing." In corporate America, Sandra struggled to find the balance of identity, self-expression, and professionally accepted behavior. The first few years were a struggle for her, and she had to learn to find the right balance. "I grew up in an environment where passion and enthusiasm were normal and celebrated, and I struggled to find balance in my culture, my identity, and this new world." Everything she had grown up with that translated to the culture in the workplace was being questioned in America, which she has now made home.

Being raised to adulthood in a different country poses a different kind of challenge for adult immigrants who step into the corporate workplace. There is a need to understand a new country as well as work culture. As Sandra described, "In Colombia, we are very passionate about everything. For example, if there is a successful project, I will give hugs to coworkers in the office. This was frowned upon and deemed inappropriate." She focused on finding a way to channel her expression into her work. "My passion helped me to figure out complex problems, and I could see this as an advantage at work." As adult immigrants in the workplace, we have existing styles and ways of work that are either resisted or welcomed in a new country. Our identities are unique, and the key is finding the right balance of what is acceptable while staying true to individual identity and style. Channeling our personality strengths and cultural background into our work styles can bring value and add to the culture of the workplace, which could lead to unique and beneficial work results.

MULTIPLE INTERSECTIONS, UNIQUE IDENTITY

"Nothing of me is original. I am the combined effort of everyone I've ever known."

—CHUCK PALAHNIUK

The topic of identity is personal. The factors that shape what it means for everyone are very different. Katya Stepanov was born in Minsk, Belarus, to a Jewish Ukrainian mother and a Russian Ukrainian father, four days after the collapse of the former Soviet Union. Identity was a topic that she's had to think about for a long time. Her mother is from the Ashkenazi Jewish lineage, whose ancestors lived in the Pale of Settlement in Eastern Europe—what is now modern-day Belarus, Poland, Ukraine, Slovenia, and parts of Moldova. Her father is from a Russian Ukrainian lineage, whose ancestors lived in various parts of Russia and Ukraine and likely had a history of serfdom. With her strong cultural attachments and history, she sums up her background as:

"Stepanov, the Russian, married Erlikh, the Jewish 'intelligentsia' girl. And I was born into this collapsing empire, which was suddenly not the USSR, but rather, Belarus."

In the 1990s, the American Jewish community was actively working in partnership with the United States government to grant asylum to Russian Jews who faced persecution during the Soviet era. Her parents were able to apply for and were granted asylum based on their Jewish heritage. The family of three, none of whom spoke any English, immigrated to the United States when Katya was a year old. "We were like, Aliens. My first ID card actually said 'resident alien,' and this is exactly how I felt."

Stepanov, with her blond hair and blue eyes, could easily blend in with Americans. However, she was also strongly connected to her cultural identities and her lineage. She grew up in a neighborhood where most of the residents were Russian Jewish immigrants who wanted to preserve their cultural lifestyle, stories, and activities. In keeping with this, they sent their children to a Russian after-school program, among many other cultural activities such as ballroom dance, piano, and advanced mathematics. The residents of the community shared a deep cultural connection as well as a history of trauma.

> "Being Russian in my town was normal. We had a Russian food store and a banya. It was a hub of all these people who all had the same shared experience of trauma and had even started a Russian cultural center in town. I didn't speak English until I went to school, and even then, Russian remained my first language at home. My household felt very post-Soviet. From a very early age, I was navigating two different realities, my household felt like we were still in Russia; everyone took their shoes off before entering, was aggressively

fed by my grandmother, and spoke Russian. While in school or with my friends, it was America, and I tried really hard to fit in until I realized the value in my unique third-culture-kid experience."

Early in her corporate career, Katya worked for a start-up company where she facilitated workshops and led motivational sessions for corporate leaders. The mostly white and male audience intimidated her. "The biggest hurdle for me to get over at first was all my complexes around why would they respect me? I'm just a five-foot-three Belarusian girl attempting to inspire this roomful of one hundred-plus white men."

As a facilitator and a team builder, Katya needed something different to find a voice and overcome the barrier to doing her job. She found a way to use the undervalued power of her uniqueness and translate it into a tool that enabled her to find her voice and thrive at work. "I realized that my uniqueness is a great bridge, especially if I can find humor about myself and draw attention to my own culture intentionally." Katya Stepanov started to intentionally put it up front, starting her speeches with a possible Russian stereotype laced with humor. "I would take the microphone, and I would be like, 'You all missed my undercover helicopter entrance into the conference room, but I'll forgive you. It's fine; it's fine.'" Katya discovered the psychological power of using humor to get through and get people prepared for her sessions, and it was a win for everyone. "It's the best way, as soon as people laugh at themselves or each other, they're able to connect. There are no borders to humor. I would just play with the stereotypes right in the beginning." From Katya's unique heritage, her journey with identity as an immigrant in America has done more than just shape her own life. It has also shaped her work, purpose, and passion. The company she founded, The Inheritance Project, focuses on training inclusive leaders through the lens of cultural and emotional inheritance. This work is the result of her journey of navigating through her identities, culture, and uniqueness, and how she converted it all into a model to help others do the same.

Our identity is from our past; our present is tomorrow's past.

THRIVING IN INTERSECTIONALITY: IDENTITY EXPRESSION IN THE WORKPLACE

The labels that people assign to us are always going to be subjective. We have no control over the origin of their labels.

Every individual has an identity journey woven into every part of our lives. As immigrants, there is a stronger awareness of that because of the process of integrating into a new environment. As an immigrant in a new workplace environment, there is a need to observe and learn. There is the country's culture, the past of the country, and the workplace culture. Blending in is not sustainable. Integration is a process that evolves over time, and it is important to recognize and hold on to our uniqueness and identity; that is what will be retained and refined in the longer term.

There is a difference between assimilation (just blending in) and integration. Integration involves finding a way to blend originality with accepting a new place. The journey in a new space requires balancing retaining our authenticity to allowing ourselves to evolve. It is not always about us. Not all spaces truly want authenticity. Find the spaces and teams that welcome authenticity.

Identity is a journey we have all already started. Accept it, explore it, and grow into it. It doesn't end in the current workplace. Our career paths are individual journeys, and they begin with our identity. It is up to us as individuals to discover that and to lean into the dimensions that help us be authentic. The label "immigrant" is only one of many dimensions. Every individual is a unique combination of many attributes. We have our skills and hobbies, our educational qualifications, our descriptors on the home front as a parent or a sibling, and our religious identities. The experiences we have had has impacted our outlook on life and shaped the way we adapt to the workplace. Everyone will have their definitions and descriptors for us based on subjective opinions. It is important to continue to be grounded in who we are and how we describe ourselves, so we can show up authentically at work.

SELF-IDENTITY CHECK-IN

- What are the identity "dimensions" that I would use to describe myself?
- How do I show up at home?
- How do I show up daily in my workplace?
- What do I feel uncomfortable sharing or showing in the workplace?
- What part of my job brings me the most joy?
- What do I frequently get feedback on?
- What aspects of my identity am I currently struggling with because I don't feel I have a safe outlet in my workplace?

EXPLORE

What opportunities exist in my organization or outside to explore the dimensions that I feel pressured to hide?

"Implicit bias—our subconscious associations of race—permeates everything that we do. And we must pursue systemic accountability to fix it."

—OPAL TOMETI

CHAPTER TWO

RACIAL EMERGENCE

INTRODUCTION

I was born and raised in Nigeria, West Africa, so I grew up among people with skin color like mine. Although I have always been a lighter-skinned in Nigeria, where there are different shades of black skin, I have always been Black. However, skin color was not really the core separator or topic of conversation in Nigeria, and "being a Black person" is different from "being Black in America." Being Black is a significant identity dimension in America, and it is worth calling out the difference because for a Black person from Africa, the cultural background and experiences are unique differences. When I started working on this book, it was not primarily because of skin color. I wanted to focus on the workplace experiences from the perspective of being the "other" at work and what that "other" means for an immigrant—just like I began to realize that the word "immigrant" in America covers a continuum. I also realized that, for immigrants, it would also sometimes be about race and how people make assumptions based on skin color without peeling back that layer and seeing the immigrant dimension that has a larger impact. The color of our skin is the first filter through which people identify us. That skin color association consciously or unconsciously comes from individual bias and stereotypes. Immigrating to America as an adult, I had to learn what blackness in America means because my skin is black, and for some people, that puts me in a certain category. This process of socialization and coming into awareness of my skin color as a Black person in America is what I describe as "racial emergence." Racial emergence is a phrase used to capture how adult immigrants gradually become aware of race and skin color in a different way from how they were raised outside of America. There is a long and deeply complicated history of race in America. Depending on where we grew up, we harbor different perspectives of America and race and only through experience—a gradual racial emergence process—can it be truly understood.

I grew up in a relatively small town, and as a middle-class family in Nigeria, we thrived on community and relationships. I went to primary school in a community where my dad worked. I went to a girls-only boarding school, and my dad was a professor at the college where I got my first degree. Even though I didn't really see a lot of female representation in the corporate workplace in my immediate environment as a child, I did have members of my extended family who are female and thriving professionals. I had never really lived the reality as the "only" or the "other" until I arrived in the United States and then started in corporate America.

The true reality of being Black in America is a lived experience. Nothing prepares an immigrant for being Black in America except being Black in America.

As part of the conversations for this book, a few immigrant women of color provided feedback on their racial emergence journey. Examining the feedback on the race perspective and specifically as non-Caucasian women, each person touched on different aspects that I wanted to highlight.

BLACK IN AMERICA
AFRICAN AND BLACK IN AMERICA

Anu Iwanefun was born and raised in Nigeria. Growing up in a country where everyone is Black, the physical color as an identity dimension is not an area of immediate awareness. After Anu immigrated as a teenager, she struggled to understand what the reference "you're Black" meant for her in America. "When you first see me and maybe potentially when you first hear me, you see me as a Black woman, right? So, the first thing you're not seeing me as is Nigerian." The identity that she had carried with her had always been Nigerian. Going into college as a Black person living in the United States shortly after her arrival, she heard a lot of questions and comments from her Black American colleagues that she did not understand. There were different comments around available opportunities. Anu also experienced different microaggressions at school that prompted an interest in seeking a better understanding of the Black American history. "I realized that being in this country, I'm going to be classified as Black first and not Nigerian."

Anu was not required to take a class in Black history, but while in college, she made a conscious decision to take it. "I wanted to learn more on the story and the history of this new identity that I was being seen as." The class on both Black history and African history was insightful for her and shed light on a lot of the issues in America and with racism. With her African American friends, Anu was able to understand a little better about the lived experiences and unpacking microaggressions. "I wanted to understand so I could better show up for myself and my friends at school and also in the workplace." Now in corporate America, she appreciates all the education that she had and the experiences that continue to educate her at work. "I always want to show up as my true self, and that includes my passion for advocacy for both immigrants, and all Blacks in the workplace."

AMERICAN AND BLACK IN AMERICA

Unlike Anu, who immigrated as a teenager, Keiko Nevers, was the only one in her family to be born in the United States. She identifies as an immigrant and describes herself as having a front-row seat to both her Black American family and Jamaican family interactions. Keiko's mom was pregnant with her when her parents and older siblings all immigrated. "I accept United States as home because I was born and raised here. I accept Jamaica as home because I was raised in a Jamaican household with a fully Jamaican family, not an American, you know, patriarch or matriarch in my family." The family settled in Gary, Indiana, a town and state where there was a clear racial divide in the 1990s. Growing up, her parents worked multiple jobs in white communities before eventually starting their own business. She saw her parents work to build the community up and lift other Blacks in the neighborhood. Education was very important to the family.

The struggles of having limited opportunities available without an education was prevalent and her family made good education a priority. "We going to get educated, we going to go into corporate America, we going to get these jobs, and we're gonna feed money back into our community." Keiko observed her father's business thrive while focused on supporting the Black community and building relationships that cut across different races. Bridging the gaps between neighborhoods and having a business that served both white and Black communities caused a lot of controversy in the '90s. In a racially divided America, even the efforts to help were viewed differently by white Americans and Black Americans. However, Keiko watched her parents persist and observed the positive outcomes that resulted. She learned the value of bridging gaps and connecting across racial divides. Now she leverages those same skills in her work leading people and programs in corporate America.

"I saw my parents networking in the community, to get customers and to maintain customers and I apply that to my corporate career. I connect with people on a real level and by the time we're done getting to know each other, they know they can trust me and they're willing to help me."

DISCRIMINATION AT HOME
RELIGIOUS MINORITY

Unlike Anu and Keiko, Yudita Markovich is an immigrant who moved as an adult from a home situation where she was a minority. She was better prepared to deal with racism and discrimination in corporate America. Yudita was born in what is now known as Western Ukraine, a region by the borders of Hungary, Romania, Slovakia, and Ukraine. "My family's Jewish, all four of my grandparents are concentration camp survivors, and where I was born, I'm a visibly identifiable ethnic other from blocks away." Being Jewish in Europe, a religious minority made her an identifiable "other" by her name and visible appearance—a group that did not belong. Yudita immigrated to the United States as a child. "I feel kinship with a lot of people. Even though it might not be obvious to them why. And then, growing up I've always been able to build relationship more closely with other immigrant children."

Working in human resources in America for the last twenty years, Yudita does a lot of interviewing and job placement in her corporate role. She describes herself as relating with the Blacks in America, the ethnic "others," and how comfortably she has defined her own style of getting to know people better through a combination of looks, language, and names. "I like when people ask me, other than be assumptive and so I do the same for my candidates. Physical is the way that other people can see. So, the optics matter." Because of her background of being a minority at home, she could relate with those that have experienced discrimination and being labeled. Yudita takes all her past experiences and uses them to shape the way she connects with candidates (especially those who belong to a minority group) and helps place them in the right roles.

ETHNIC MINORITY

Khady Gaye is a Black woman who was born and raised in Belgium. In the bilingual country, she grew up speaking the two main languages, Dutch and French. Although she was born in Belgium, her parents were immigrants from Senegal. Before she immigrated to the United States almost two years ago, she describes her experience growing up as a citizen of the world. At nine years old, she had a teacher humiliate her and strike her in front of the entire class: "He looked me in the eyes and said, 'Oh, but you know, with your skin, you have a thick skin, so you don't feel the pain, right?'"

As a Black European, Khady has had to toughen up against macro acts of racism in society. From her childhood, she has had to learn to confront people as well as educate others within the systems as she moved along within the corporate workplace. Starting her career in Europe, she describes the constant challenges brought about by the assumptions that because she is Black, she has the menial roles within the team. "I started as a sales assistant. And then I quickly realized that translation was not my thing or wanting to have more social interactions. So, I moved into human resources."

She had a master's degree and had advanced in the corporate world. However, she continued to get the assumption from people that she had a lesser role. "I work for an airline company and generally during networking, the first assumption is like, 'Oh, you're a flight attendant?' and I am like, 'No, I am a human resources manager.'"

Getting her first job in Europe was not difficult because she was bilingual, and that was a big advantage in the country. However, it becomes insufficient as you advance. "When you want to look for a higher-level position, then suddenly, being bilingual is not enough. You are on the shortlist, and if they must make the choice between two equal candidates, then the color of my skin comes to play. Maybe that is the reason why I immigrated from Belgium to the US."

For Khady, who already grew up as an ethnic minority in Europe, immigrating to the United States was an easier experience for her. She found it easier to get settled and thrive in corporate America. "In the US, you can see Black people in senior leadership positions, even if it's a very low percentage it does exist. In Europe, in most of the companies, there are none." After successfully building a twenty-year career, she learned not to accept defeat and carried the attitude into her job in corporate America leading human resources. Embracing her identity and describing herself as a citizen of the world, Khady learned that trying to fit into a mold from others can become a chore to try and please people.

"I have already learned to strengthen my muscles and to be proud of who I am. I always say that I'm not there to fit. I think your shoes or your clothes need to fit because you have a certain morphology that allows you to wear a certain size, and your feet should match with the size of shoes. But other than that, it's not about fitting into a box."

Like Khady, if you are an immigrant woman in corporate America with preexisting experience associated with racial discrimination, you are better equipped and have more confidence to deal with racist actions. It doesn't make you immune, but it does help you to respond better and continue to advance and thrive in corporate America.

Finally, the topic of blending depends on the length of time and location as well. For Khady Gaye, who was born in Belgium, immigrating to the United States was relatively easy. As a Black person born to an immigrant family in Europe, she describes herself as having already integrated and developed a thick skin. When she immigrated to the United States, she had gone through multiple global roles and organizations and found her voice in the workplace. "I have learned to strengthen my muscles and to be proud of who I am. It's not about fitting into a box. It's about what you bring to the table. What do you value? How do your values match with those of the company?"

THRIVING IN INTERSECTIONALITY: IMMIGRANTS AND RACE IN AMERICA

"It is not our differences that divide us. It is our inability to recognize, accept, and celebrate those differences."

—AUDRE LORDE

Being an immigrant, a woman, and a Black person in America creates a new intersection with the multiplied impact in the workplace. When an individual has all three dimensions, which was the case for most of the women I spoke with for this book, it creates an amplification of the negative impact of a single underrepresented dimension from bias and stereotypes. The context of this book is corporate America with its own policies and processes that a lot of the time fall short of being inclusive of all employees. For immigrants, having answers to the questions on identity and Blackness in America has an impact on the company culture and policies for creating spaces where immigrants belong. We start with the individuals who are at the immigrant intersection, getting to a place where they feel empowered and confident at work. Then, the collective voices of underrepresented individuals who learn to stand against oppression, discrimination, and exclusion for all can drive the change that we need to make corporate cultures more inclusive.

According to the Pew Research Center, the number of immigrants in the United States has grown significantly over the last two decades. In addition, immigrants are a growing part of the American corporate and technical skilled workforce. Immigrants can be a strong part of the American and race story, but it starts with learning where we all started and what we have not been a part of. The focus on immigrants within the corporate workforce in this book is important because we need to highlight the different journeys and experiences to understand race in America. As we address the barriers to integration in the workplace, there is also an opportunity to incorporate education for immigrants at work.

When the focus is primarily on the physical perspective of skin color, it does not allow for the inclusion of our different cultural perspectives. Depending on how long an immigrant has lived in the US and what part of the country they were raised in, there is a growing awareness of the color filter in America. This culture impacts us all, and changes need to involve everyone.

POINTS TO THINK ABOUT:
- As a Black immigrant or immigrant of color, what is my perspective on race in America?
- How can I continue to learn?
- What privilege do I have because of how I was raised?
- How can I be an ally for other immigrants, Blacks, and/ or people of color at work?
- Where can I add my voice to make a difference?

SECTION II

STEPPING INTO CORPORATE AMERICA

"No one leaves home, unless home is the mouth of a shark"

—WARSAN SHIRE

CHAPTER THREE

LEGAL BARRIERS

INTRODUCTION

Getting a college degree involves overcoming different barriers—even in your birth country. In Nigeria, the main obstacles are passing the qualifying examinations to get in and then financing your education one school term after another. While not a guarantee of an immediate job, getting a degree gives you a competitive advantage over those without a degree. In Nigeria, if finances are not an issue, students go through high school and full-time undergraduate college programs before starting to look for their first job. After my undergraduate program, I worked for two years before coming in to start my master's program on a student visa. There are different immigrant and non-immigrant visa categories for getting into the Unites States; each comes with different restrictions. In my case, I came to the United States as an international student on an F-1 student visa. The student visa gave me the authorization to work for only twenty hours on a campus job during my program. With an international student status, the high tuition rates, and the cost of living, twenty hours of a campus job is never sufficient for bills. There is an opportunity to apply for internships after the first year, but it must be directly aligned with the degree of record on the visa. The few opportunities that are available are always very competitive. This means the search for full-time jobs starts very early and dropping out of school is not an option. Legal visa status depends on staying in school and passing.

Once I fully began my job search, the rejections started rolling in. I found one of the popular feedback items that the recruiters pointed to was "a lack of work experience," even for roles that required no advanced degree. As a master's degree holder with two years of work experience, I expected that I would be very qualified for entry-level positions. What I later got to understand was that seeing the international experience and education on my resume created a barrier regarding work-visa sponsorship. Not many organizations are capable of or even willing to sponsor a work visa processing for candidates transitioning from international student status. So, it wasn't just a search for the right role aligned with the student visa category; it was for the organization that was familiar with the H-1B visa process and willing to employ an international student including being qualified and resourced for the visa sponsorship process. The other unsaid reality is that your work experience outside of the United States, especially as an early-stage career professional, was not seen as valid. So even though I had an advanced degree and a little bit of experience, I learned to begin to expand my applications to roles that required no advanced degree. It was a combination of factors for me, and every immigrant story is different, but this highlights just some of the different barriers to entry that immigrants face getting in and starting out in corporate America, even with the skills and certifications.

THE GRADUATE STUDENT VISA BARRIER

Darshini Mehta immigrated to the United States at age twenty-seven after obtaining her doctoral degree in biochemistry from India. She came in with the goal of securing a post-doc position. However, even for American citizens, getting a postdoc position is very difficult. As an immigrant, the competition is even stiffer because the qualifications you have earned outside the US are not always recognized at the same level. This put her at a disadvantage competing for postdoctoral positions when she arrived in the United States. She received offers for positions as a technician, but this is a lower-level job, and she knew she was overqualified for these sorts of roles. As an international postdoc applicant, Mehta came in well-educated but competed for limited spots.

"As immigrants, highly educated immigrants, we are starting from ground zero without our peer networks in the United States."

In addition to missing the network and peer connections, another area of distinction for immigrants is their visa status. The immigrant visa categories are very different for entry into the United States, with each of them bearing different restrictions. Each visa type and category comes with a time limit on staying without a job as well as a restriction on what types of jobs you can take. Depending on the visa stipulations, only certain companies and certain roles are valid for staying within legal status. Fortunately for Darshini, after choosing to decline the technician roles and holding out, she eventually successfully secured a postdoc position. Getting into the postdoc program, she encountered the harsh reality of the hectic work and minimal pay.

A 2020 survey of over seven thousand postdocs across ninety-three nations shows a trend of growing dissatisfaction among academic postdoc researchers. Despite the long hours, another area of frustration is also the lack of appropriate recognition for work done. Postdoc research work tends to get assigned to the longest-tenured person in the lab to get the first authorship for the work produced. This meant that the recognition was not based on your hard work; it was based on rank. This meant even though Darshini was working very hard and long hours, the recognition was going to the highest-ranking person in the lab, who also happened to have been there the longest, in her case.

When Mehta had her first child during her postdoc program, it became difficult to maintain the work hours and schedule. She made adjustments to get all her work done, but she couldn't work the same hours as everyone else, socialize after work, or work weekend hours like everyone else. Her husband was also a postdoc, and they didn't have any family support in the United States.

"We were in that boat where we were thinking, 'We have to go back because we were not sure our visa would come through.' The postdoc visa is only for a certain period. It doesn't get converted into H-1 work visa until you get a qualifying job."

For immigrants in a postdoc program, the option becomes staying on in the postdoc program with minimal pay, without funding or advancement, while continuing to put in the long hours but enjoying full benefits and visa security. Alternatively, immigrants start to think about the options available in corporate roles or teaching opportunities. It is a time-sensitive call because whatever options get selected, the visa status needs to be sponsored and usually allows for a limited number of years of stay in the United States.

"Luckily, there was a different category available for my husband. There was the work that he was doing that qualified him for a green card because of the very specific work that put him in a special category."

Ultimately for Darshini Mehta and her family, it wasn't the hard work under hectic conditions with no support that helped. Even with multiple degrees, they were at risk of having to return home to start over. Darshini described what helped as "luck." They were privileged to be able to leverage the best of both visas waiting for a qualifying job. Darshini was eventually able to make a move into a biotechnology company as a technical support scientist starting a career that has spanned more than two decades.

"As an immigrant, even if you have a whole string of degrees, at the initial applicant level, your resumes are screened out for lower roles. Even if you would have gladly taken these roles because of visa needs and the time-sensitive requirements. However, you also do not qualify for a senior-level position because you have never had a valid work experience in the US."

Darshini is now a senior leader at a global biotechnology company. In those early years of her career, she described how much of her focus was not on advancing but on staying in. Even while learning a new job and company culture, the larger pressure was on staying within the legal requirements.

"I grew up where it was more, you're just following the teacher, and you're not challenging them." Darshini eventually got settled and had to learn to find the opportunities to grow her career within the organization. Presenting and defending her qualifications and accomplishments did not come naturally to her, and she has had to pick what battles were worth fighting along the way. But getting the confidence to make her interest known to her managers, applying for roles where she could make contributions in her workspaces, and still stay within status have all been instrumental in growing her career.

THE ORGANIZATION VISA PROCESSING BARRIER

Unlike Darshini, Rachel Rudo came to the US after high school to pursue a college education. However, she knew she was at a disadvantage without experience, and so she came determined to find some work experience before she graduated. She was on a college scholarship from Zimbabwe and was excited to immigrate and make the most of the opportunity to build a career. As the first of four kids, her goal was to graduate quickly and get an excellent paying job to support her parents. Armed with that determination, she intentionally got a campus job at the library so she could use her breaks to search for internships. Every day during her break, she would send a letter to a company that she has identified as a leader in the market research space, her academic area. Her emails had a similar message: "I would love some experience. I would love to intern with you. I'll intern for free I want to learn more about market research. Please hire me as your intern. I know my resume doesn't say much but trust me, if you meet me, you will hire me on the spot."

Rachel faxed a cover letter out every day to a new company for a whole month until she eventually received a call asking to come in for an interview. "They hired me on the spot, and then they said, 'And we have something else to tell you. We're gonna pay you!' It was amazing. I started working there as an intern but a paid intern." Working as a paid intern was a dream come true, and she was working in a company aligned with her interest. The company eventually offered her a full-time position after graduation with an offer to sponsor her work visa. Not every company was able to sponsor a work visa. Considering this was an additional requirement that immigrants must consider in the job search, she was excited to start work post-graduation.

However, the problems started when she sensed delays and issues with her work visa processing. Although it was a dream team, company, and job for her, she started having concerns about how the human resources (HR) and legal teams were handling her work permit. She expressed her concerns to HR when she was not getting sufficient updates, and they provided vague confirmations. Unfortunately for her, the process was utterly mismanaged. The right filing paperwork was delayed passed the required deadline for her to be in status. She became out of legal status, and the company asked her to stay home while they promised to sort it out. She was home waiting without pay for three months before they had to officially let her go, and by then, her status had expired, and she was in a legal bind.

For Rachel, the errors and delays with her filings were the beginning of a ten-year legal battle with the United States immigration and legal systems. For someone who wanted to support her family, she ended up in a position where she had to leverage her family's financial support to handle the legal fees and processes while she went through multiple court hearings and job status. Living in the United States away from her family, she was grateful she had their support both emotionally and financially throughout the process.

A lot of immigrant students do not have the immigration knowledge nor the financial backing to handle issues around visa or hire legal representation. Unfortunately, the companies do not always have the right resources to support job candidates on immigrant visas. This means most organizations shy away from considering international students or candidates with an immigrant visa requirement, or they leave the document handling to the candidate. This places immigrants in a difficult position when applying for and accepting jobs.

Similar to Rachel Rudo, Shevonne Dyer was born and raised in Trinidad and Tobago and came to the United States in 2008 on a student visa for college. A few weeks before she completed her master's program in industrial and organizational psychology, she was excited to receive a confirmed job offer from a top firm in the United States. This was an exciting position to be in because the job closely aligned with the program she studied, and it met the requirement for her legally required optional practical training (OPT): finding a job within ninety days of its start.

Shevonne got her orientation welcome package, followed by instructions to take a drug test. She thought little of it and showed up at the facility with minimal understanding of the company's policy. This was when she was informed that the drug test involved getting a sample of her hair. Right there, she made the decision to have a lock of her hair cut from her scalp. However, soon after she made this sacrifice, she got disappointing news just before she was scheduled to start her new role. "I got an email saying that the program is no longer funded, and the position is no longer available." Shevonne was confused and disappointed. Because she had gotten an offer and a confirmation, she had stopped looking for a job and now had to scramble to find a qualifying job before her work permit expired.

At the last minute, she got referred for a job interview for an HR clerk position. She saw some red flags during the interview that spoke to toxicity at work and she knew the job was below her qualifications, but all of these were irrelevant at this point as she was desperate to find a job before she fell out of immigration status. "After I eventually got hired and started work, I realized that little bit of condescension I had noticed during my interview with the hiring manager, transferred from the interview to our daily interactions." Shevonne described different instances of microaggressions from her manager with her daily job. "I would stay back and work extra to get my job done, but when I put in the hours it was an issue to bill for overtime. I was working hard, saving the company money, but I was criticized for my boss's errors." Fortunately for her, she found a mentor internally who supported her and would give her those teaching moments to foster her professional growth and development. She also looked for a leader in the company who was familiar with her immigration situation to gain their support and understanding toward continued employment possibilities.

The pressure of trying to scramble for a job within the legal requirements can lock an immigrant into the wrong company culture or leave them working for a toxic manager. Getting in can be hard, but once you are in, it is important to find a safe person to share with and understand the internal options available. Avoiding internalized criticisms can be difficult, but with the right mentors and sponsors, we can learn and grow while in a job we need to stay in for a period.

THE EMPLOYEE VISA BARRIER TO GROWTH

Immigrants face multiple legal restrictions and barriers to getting into the corporate workplace, and these legal barriers can also limit growth. Even with prior work experience, people have fewer opportunities to translate the prior experiences into a current job. This was the case for Rekha Prodduturi, who was born and raised in India. Although she had prior work experience with a track record of success, she still had legal visa restrictions. Rekha got married and had a child as a career mom in India while she grew her career in the global mobility industry. She had been to the United States a few times and never really considered leaving India until she was recruited for a job in the United States. After some consideration, she decided to immigrate with her family for the job.

Although Rekha did not have any issues with the visa processing step (as her company handled everything appropriately), she still had limitations on the type of jobs she could express interest in after a few years. As the main visa holder in the family, she had her family as her legal dependents. This meant she was conscious of the responsibility and careful about putting everyone in her family at risk. There were internal and external project opportunities that she had to decline because they might conflict with her visa specifications, and she always had to think about that from the start. This is a different type of barrier to growth and development due to legal status.

"Immigration is the sincerest form of flattery."

—JACK PAAR

THRIVING IN INTERSECTIONALITY, LEGALLY

According to the QS World University Rankings, American institutions continue to dominate, taking the top position, with a large percentage of US colleges making the top one hundred. This means that although international students are charged a higher tuition, the opportunity to study in the United States is still attractive enough for a large number of student visa applications to be issued every year to students from all over the world. Although this means the United States has the academic facilities to welcome many immigrants through the student route, less effort goes into hiring and retaining these talents in the corporate workplace. I had the privilege of getting a sponsored green card right after college, and that changed things for me. First, I had the luxury of waiting to find a job. For immigrants on student visas, there is usually a fixed time to get hired (about ninety days). Although I did get a minimum wage job in the required time frame—which was part-time and in a different industry—it ultimately took me almost five months to find a full-time "qualified" position in my industry. Secondly, I was able to update my resume to indicate "no visa sponsorship required," and that was when I started to get more responses to my applications.

There are highly qualified immigrants who come into the United States or grow up in the United States expecting to get a job and put in the work to get compensated. Depending on the visa status and route of entry, it can become discouraging to discover all the barriers that come with each step starting from job applications, the day-to-day experiences at work, and then the limitations surrounding the pursuit of growth opportunities in the workplace.

Stay informed, know your status, and know your rights. Career growth is always possible.

POINTS TO THINK ABOUT:
- Understand your specific visa requirement and limitations.
- Research the types of roles you can safely apply for within and outside your organizations.
- Connect on forums and networks to meet with other immigrants with the same status and learn.
- Join organizations that provide support and education specifically for the immigrant professional population.
- Within your organization, find immigrant mentors that can support your journey as an immigrant in the workplace.

- Volunteer, job shadow, and explore other roles before making any decisions.
- You can still focus on growth and development even as an immigrant on a work visa by taking advantage of free resources, mentors, and community programs.

"We spend far too much of our lives at work to have it be in opposition to the person we desire to be."

—SCOTT HAMMERLE

CHAPTER FOUR

CAREER CHOICES

INTRODUCTION

Some teenagers have clear career interests and paths by the time they get into college; I was not one of them. I knew the subjects I enjoyed, but I wasn't passionate about a specific job, nor did I have a clear path mapped out when college applications were due. I was in science classes, and I had good grades in the core science subjects. Since my dad was a college professor, I also had the privilege of my parents supporting the decision-making process. In Nigeria, there are very few careers that are well known and highly respected for a science-based education—namely medicine and engineering. Every parent with children performing great in sciences attempted to steer them toward medical school or engineering. I was not particularly excited about any of the two, but I loved biology and was happy to choose the medical route. I went in for biochemistry for my bachelor's with the goal of getting into medical school down the road. I realized I was not interested in going into medicine sometime during my five years of undergraduate school, and I am grateful my parents supported that as well.

My career in the corporate world started in Nigeria with an internship program in a brewing company. As a part of my college program, every student was required to take a term off and complete a six-month internship program. This was an educational part of our curriculum, and we came back for the final year to deliver a report on the internship experience. During my internship, I was assigned to a quality lab, and for the first five months, I got to run daily tests on in-process products and deliver samples. However, my favorite part of the six months was the final month. It was rotation style, and I got to work in the different parts of the brewery for a few days at a time. Getting to spend a few days in a different part of the brewery gave me a good understanding of each department's inputs and outputs and how the internal process chain was connected. I got a different kind of exposure to career opportunities and roles and realized a project style of work might work better for me than one requiring repetitive tasks. Many of my roles have been project-based, and for each new project that I get to explore, I love the excitement and the new people I get to meet. I could not have predicted my corporate career path, but every time I have made a change, I always make sure there will be an opportunity to gain new knowledge.

PASSION AND FINDING CAREER PATH

For Jaya Mallik, a first-generation American from India, her cultural and community upbringing did successfully influence her career path in a way that might not be immediately obvious. Growing up in DC, her childhood neighborhood had about eleven different members of her extended family living within a mile of each other. They leaned on and supported each other within the geographical community.

She grew up learning to value having community and the importance of keeping it. "Families in our culture are multigenerational and tend to live very closely together. My definition of an immediate family is inclusive of all my extended family members." The definition of community and family also means being responsible for and caring for each other. These cultural, community, and family orientations have also shaped her work. "The choices I've made professionally in terms of what roles I have taken, what career paths I have pursued, have all been focused on community."

Jaya started her career in teaching. As a teacher, she thought of the type of community in which she grew up and recognized that opportunity was not equally distributed to different children. She wanted to make communities better for families like hers. She was passionate about the communities she got to serve through her work. "I wanted to impact the kids and provide more opportunities for the neighborhoods where opportunities are not readily available." When she eventually moved into a corporate role, she significantly saw a need to impact developing communities through learning and development efforts. As an employee within people operations, she loves working in positions where she impacts the experiences of individuals and teams as they show up at work every day.

"My family was always focused on we are better 'as a whole' than separated; we're better and stronger together than apart. So, when we come together and we help each other, we all thrive."

She acknowledges the impact of the community she grew up in, the relationships, and the special interactions between her extended family members involved in her upbringing, providing her the stability and the resilience needed in her career. In her different roles, she also wants to be a part of helping employees thrive within corporate organizations.

"I want to be a part of making it safe for people to bring themselves fully to work and to bring their ideas safely so our corporate communities can thrive."

As an immigrant, Jaya's background has continued to guide her career choices and the value she brings to her different roles. She has taken roles where she feels that connection and purpose of impacting teams and groups. Her background has become a guiding light that she gets to lean into to find belonging and joy in her jobs. She is currently in a role as a part of the diversity, equity, and inclusion team at a biotechnology company. "I feel a sense of fulfillment from striving to help everyone find the sense of community to show up at work and continuing to drive changes that impact others."

Although Jaya would not say she had a clear career path when she was young, she looks back now and sees how her path had been shaped by her upbringing. She was able to steer her career in the direction of interest based on her background and her passions and clarified her path as she advanced.

PROVING QUALIFICATION AND BUILDING CAREER

As an immigrant, even when your career path and interests are clear, sometimes there is the need to prove yourself and defend your skills at work. For Mercedes Soria, when she immigrated to the US from South America to study computer science, it was with a scholarship for her desired program. After earning both her bachelor's and a master's degree in computer science, she embarked on a tedious job search process. With her skills and qualifications, she didn't expect to have a hard time getting a job in her field of study. "I applied to more than one hundred different companies; only three of those called me back in for an interview. And of those three, only one offered me an actual job."

As a master's degree holder, the one job offer Mercedes finally got was website maintenance, one that had no degree requirement. However, she had no choice but to accept, especially since they offered to process her paperwork conversion from a student visa F-1 to a work visa. As discussed in chapter three, getting into corporate America on a student visa carries two main legal limits along with it: time (ninety days after graduation) and relevance to the degree category. So, although Mercedes realized she was overqualified for the job and it was a role below her expectation, she was grateful that one company took a chance on her and gave her the initial opportunity to get into corporate America.

Once Mercedes got in, she started to explore different internal opportunities to use her skills. She made an early discovery that the internal computer systems the company used were outdated. Recognizing the opportunity, she took on the task of working on upgrades whenever she had time. "I ended up building all the internal systems based on emerging web technologies." She found ways to do the work that she had been educated for and practiced by solving problems within the company. In addition, she researched ways to get up to speed on new skills. She found the right computer technology conferences and submitted requests for sponsorship to attend.

As a female engineer and an immigrant working in Silicon Valley, Mercedes also found she was the "other" and the "only" in the room in a lot of cases. Although she had the degrees and loved computer engineering, she realized getting those degrees and getting the job was only the beginning of an uphill battle. She still had to fight individual assumptions and look for ways to show her capabilities as a woman in a male-dominated career. Earlier in her career, she was promoted along with three other peers. One of her coworkers stopped at her desk to congratulate her and make a comment: "The only reason why you were promoted is not that you're good or because you know anything. You were only promoted because you're a minority, you're in technology, and you're a woman."

The insinuation was that Mercedes was not deserving of the promotion based on her skills but simply to help the organization boost the diversity numbers. Having people question your competency in the corporate world can be overwhelming. Mercedes discovered that, while having the education and the degrees are important, they do not guarantee a great corporate job. "The good thing about having enough experience now is that with twenty years in the industry, I know what I'm doing, and then if somebody tells me that I don't, I have the knowledge myself and the self-confidence to say, 'You're wrong.'"

As an immigrant and a woman, you question yourself on the reasons behind other people's biased behaviors. "You have to do a lot of mental processing every day." It could be because you're female or an immigrant—or because of both. Mercedes learned to be patient and find the right opportunities to show her skills. Even when you get the jobs you desire that are in your field of study, as an immigrant, as a woman, and as an individual with multiple intersections, not all people will appreciate that. Immigrants are not usually prepared for this reality. The mental stress of living under a system where you feel like you need to prove yourself. Today Mercedes Soria is still in Silicon Valley thriving as a part of the founding team of Knightscope, Inc., a start-up that went public in 2022.

EVOLVED CAREER PATH

For Slavica Tomic, her path was not clear from the start. Born and raised in Bosnia, her career started in 2000 in Bosnia at an American company. She spoke very little English and did not have any degree when she started. "I got hired in a small department that took care of soldiers and their well-being in a foreign country." She was content to do her job and make her living in the role she had for a while. "I grew up in a country where we did not have plenty of options. Once you get a job, that's it, for the rest of your life."

That mentality guided her for the first two years of her career, where she just wanted to get her job done. She didn't have any plans on moving or changing roles. But she had a friend who worked in the finance department who invited and encouraged her to take on a different role in the finance department. "I had no knowledge of accounting/finance processes, no college degree, and definitely did not understand how to match invoices to the PO." With her friend's encouragement, Slavica got in, learned the job within two weeks, and then filled in while her friend went on vacation. "To be honest, that helped me a lot in boosting my confidence. I learned something, right there and then, that we can do anything if we set our minds to it. From that point on I was not afraid of stepping out of my comfort zone." In the temporary role, Slavica got to learn a lot about the finance process by doing it for an extended period. "I learned accounts payable, accounts receivable, dealing with cash, and ended up being a payroll processing analyst for the company at the time."

Slavica discovered the power of learning and got intentional about looking for opportunities to learn new things. She realized it was not about knowing everything 100 percent, but being willing to step out of her comfort zone and learn. When an opportunity opened in the Middle East, she stepped up and worked on a global project for the company.

Eventually, an opportunity came up to work on a project in the United States in support of a project that involved the current enterprise resource planning (ERP) system at the company. "I didn't know a lot about the ERP system at that point but was very interested and agreed to immigrate to the United States for the role and project." Slavica stepped into an opportunity that opened a new line of career, exposure, and learning. "I fell in love with the ERP systems and grew my understanding of how the operations runs and the thoughtful policies and procedures that are needed to support."

The project participation helped her learn a lot about the business operations and get a better perspective on how things work and the opportunities and roles available. Once she moved to the United States, she applied to a college to get her degree while continuing to work full time. She got an opportunity to join the audit department and took it.

After twenty-two years in the same company, Slavica has moved through various roles and departments. She advanced her career by being willing to take the risk and stepping out of her comfort zone, which opened the next door for opportunities while allowing her to find her passion along the way. Coming from a place at the beginning of her journey, where she was content with where she was, to a place where she has grown professionally and personally. The growth has now helped to have clearer goals. As immigrants, the value of exploring the choices and options available within the organization while engaging the support of mentors can be a great way to learn and grow in a corporate workplace. Slavica summarizes, "A few years ago, I didn't know where my career was going to take me what I wanted to do if you ask me this question. Now, I have a vision, I want to be a VP of audit one day and not just one day, in the next five years. So, I'm preparing myself to get it."

CAREER GUIDANCE ADVANTAGE

The career path looks different for everyone. For an immigrant with both parents in academia, Susan Oguche (who was introduced in chapter one) didn't have a lot of exposure to corporate work or a different career path. In her immigrant circle of Nigerian parents, kids are typically expected to go the professional career routes like medicine or engineering. However, she knew early on that she was not interested in either route. Fortunately, her parents supported her.

They helped find an internship program called INROADS. As Susan described:

"It wasn't just the internship itself, which was very cool. But throughout the summer, once a week on the weekends, there is a requirement that you go, and you get trained. It was a little annoying, because you're a kid, and especially as you get into college, you want to spend your summer having fun, but it was such an enriching experience."

She had the consistency in a company and got into her work routine early. Having the program network also helped her get a head start on professional development and an existing network of mentors that she built in her four years in the program. This program, a pathway for a minority to get a sponsor company and leverage ongoing internships program with weekend trainings, was transformational giving her a head start in her corporate career.

"Both my parents were in academia, you go do your PhD and then you know, work to get tenure and research and all these things. And this internship program just showed me a different path to being successful."

DISCOVERY JOURNEY: IDENTITY AND CAREER

For Nancy Luong, a daughter of immigrant parents from Vietnam, her goal was just to get her education. Her parents immigrated during the Vietnam War and left by boat from Vietnam to a refugee camp in Indonesia. They had escaped with their family, including their one-year-old baby, and lived in the refugee camp for two years. They had their second daughter while staying at the camp. After getting sponsored by a church in Virginia, they finally were able to leave the refugee camp and move to the US. "Where I grew up was mainly minorities. I grew up in a Hispanic area, so mainly Mexicans, and there were some Asians, some White. I would say that area was very diverse." Nancy grew up observing her parents working multiple jobs to make ends meet, but they always came home to make dinner. "We had a lot of home cooked meals, and I don't think we ever went out to eat until I was a teenager." In addition, Nancy's family had a stand at the flea market, where they worked every weekend for over twenty years. "My parents modeled hard work, and they always made it clear that they wanted all their children to get a good education, do better than they did and get good jobs."

Nancy Luong did complete her college education successfully at age twenty-two and landed a corporate job. She loved having a nice job and was content to come as far as she had. She translated a lot of the work ethics she had observed as a child and settled in with gratitude at her job. "All those years working at the flea market, all those years of hard work—I was just happy to work at a nice, fancy office with people I like."

After a while, she realized she was good at following the rules, working hard, and expressing gratitude for whatever she got, but she was not comfortable asking for things. "I didn't think I needed or even thought to ask for a raise or promotion because I did not want to jeopardize my nice job." Fortunately, Nancy had some good managers who saw her potential and moved her up the corporate ladder. While she loved her job, she realized she also wanted her job because of stability and security. "I eventually started realizing I spent so much time being grateful and keeping my head down. I was just ticking off these boxes and knew I wanted to do more."

Part of the journey has taken Nancy back to digging back into her childhood. Having conversations with her parents and her siblings and getting a new perspective to the situation and life they lived as immigrants. She has been leaning more into her identity and discovering new strengths. She also just released her first book, *How We Got Here*, in 2021, where she explores journaling and storytelling for immigrants. She describes the writing process as taking some time because she wanted to do it herself. In the journey of writing the book, she had discovered that she was getting to know herself and find her own voice. For Nancy, where she is now is satisfied and free. "While I love my job and still work, it was such a freeing experience to write and continue to write about my family's stories. I have other passions that I love and appreciate. I now know and believe I am not a burden to anyone. I don't have a fear of being fired or not good enough and I deserve to be here."

THRIVING IN INTERSECTIONALITY: CAREER EVOLUTION

As immigrants, regardless of our entry point and our corporate career track, progress can look different. Sometimes it might require changing roles, industries, or companies if legal status permits. Other times the available options might only allow for taking stretch roles at the same job or organization that we love while pursuing our passion at the side. Whatever path we choose, what is important to note is that we have choices. Defining what success means to us is a personal step but one we can be reminded that it is okay to take.

Progress starts with taking each step forward, so we can see further to the next opportunity.

Over the last decade, my corporate career in America has taken me across multiple departments and functions. As I reflect on the different titles I have earned and the roles I have held, none of these could have been planned out by my teenage self. A few of the women in this chapter mention supportive managers and mentors, and we will explore that further in chapter eight. What has been the constant is the willingness to stretch and learn new things, especially in a different country with different programs and role opportunities available. For immigrants, sometimes the degree we have can be from limited available options or a background that creates a specific focus. If we are fortunate to be able to start with our passions, we can continue to explore. In corporate America, it is important to understand these different choices and routes for career growth. Learning and development take extra effort, but with patience and determination, we can forge our paths to where we find authenticity and fulfillment in the workplace.

POINTS TO THINK ABOUT
- What have been my favorite roles?
- What made these my favorite roles?
- Outside of my job, what do I enjoy doing?
- Who caooooooor this year?
- How can I engage my managers and my community to learn and develop?

SECTION III

LIVING CORPORATELY AS AN IMMIGRANT

"The single biggest problem in communication is the illusion that it has taken place."

—GEORGE BERNARD SHAW

CHAPTER FIVE

COMMUNICATION

INTRODUCTION

In the fall of 2009, just a couple of days after I arrived in the United States for the first time, I walked down to the nearest grocery store to buy a few items. I was finding it difficult to locate a particular item, and I ended up walking up to the clerk to get some assistance. The response I got was a confused look, and then she finally said she couldn't understand me. After adjusting my volume and repeating myself a few times, I eventually walked away. My first language is Yoruba, one of the multiple languages spoken in Nigeria. However, if you are educated, English is the primary language for education, so I have been able to speak English for most of my life. That grocery trip stuck with me because it was the first time it really dawned on me that although I do speak English, it was not just about the language. Communication was more than that. I had a different accent, and that made me different.

I did eventually get comfortable with conveying my messages during the sixteen months I spent in my Texas graduate school. However, getting out of graduate school and into corporate America brought a new level of awareness. In addition to getting out of the now familiar academic space, I had also relocated from Houston, Texas, to San Diego, California. That self-consciousness and awareness of speaking differently started all over again, this time in the workplace. In the early years of my corporate career, this was a small circle of coworkers. I was in a technical role, and I didn't have to engage as much outside of my immediate team. I focused on getting clear on my deliverables, getting aligned with my manager, and delivering excellent results. As I advanced and started to work on projects across multiple functions, it became more of a job requirement to communicate often and clearly across diverse teams. Although I enjoyed speaking and had a little bit of an extrovert side, I realized I had developed a consciousness around my English pronunciation and accent that held me back from being fully present. I was not alone, and I have stories from women immigrants who felt the same way at work—women who also struggled with the impact of communication barriers at work as immigrants.

"Good communication is the bridge between confusion and clarity."

—NAT TURNER

VERBAL COMMUNICATION

Speaking with different accents is something that happens even across the same country. However, the internalized aspect of speaking differently can become the first major barrier and basis of exclusion in the corporate world. Let's take Rajal Ganatra, an immigrant to the United States from India, as an example. She explained:

"I was kind of shy and had that fear of not being fluent enough in English to express my thoughts and ideas. I was always very conscious that someone is going to either make fun of me or is going to think that I don't even speak proper English."

Rajal was born and raised in Gujarati, India. She completed her education up to a degree in chemical engineering in India. Six months after she got married, her husband got a consulting job in the United States, and they both immigrated. She was not originally authorized to work and took the opportunity to return to school and obtain another degree in biotechnology before starting her corporate career in America. Although Rajal considered herself an excellent English speaker before coming to the United States, speaking up was difficult for her at work when she first started. English was not her first language, which created many self-doubts, causing her to hold herself back from making individual contributions at work. However, refraining from speaking was not something she could continue for too long. She needed to be able to confidently speak up at work as a part of her daily role. "At work, I had to give regular briefs for a few minutes to individuals or speak in front of an audience." Since her role required such frequent speaking, she realized the self-doubts she felt could hold back her career and impact her performance at work.

Like Rajal, when my roles required speaking up and voicing my opinions, I had also found myself holding back contributions at work and critically assessing every thought. As an immigrant with a "different" accent, it is not just in the spoken words but also in the meaning of the words and questioning if the intent is captured appropriately when a suggestion is voiced in the workplace.

Rajal Ganatra and I had something in common: We both took action to improve so we could deliver the results needed to advance at work. We both joined Toastmasters to develop in an area that we recognized as very critical to success at work. The Toastmasters Club meetings provided a safe space for practicing speaking skills, with a focus on feedback and improvement—getting better. Recognizing there was a communication barrier was only the first step. Being bold enough to take small steps in doing something about it is next. This is the beginning of building back the confidence that is eroded when you stand out at work based on the way you speak.

Even with a group like Toastmasters, the improvement is gradual. As Rajal describes,

"Initially, with the Toastmasters Club, even if there were only four or five people in the club, or maybe ten people in the club, it was such a challenge for me on stage that I would literally choke and couldn't speak a single word properly."

To overcome verbal communication barriers, progress comes from consistence practice in a safe space.

Although verbal communication barriers are usually associated with specific geographic regions, that is not always accurate. Immigrants can move across multiple locations while retaining their original languages and culture. Depending on how long people stay at a certain location, they might adopt a new language and maintain the unique local dialect as well. This was the case with Paru Radia.

Paru Radia was born and raised in England, but her first language was not English. Her first language was Gujarati. This is because her family had originally immigrated from India. Her grandparents immigrated from India to Kenya. Although Paru's parents were born and raised in Kenya and her brother was also born in Kenya, the family moved to England just before she was born. As immigrants in Kenya, the family lived in an Indian community and spoke Gujarati primarily, so her parents only spoke minimal English. Growing up in England, Paru's primary language was Gujarati at home and British English in school. She stated: "I speak English, but I think in Gujarati sometimes."

Because of the multiple languages, Paru learned early on to be clear in her speaking. She had to think and then translate the appropriate words and language depending on who she was talking to. Switching frequently between both languages is more challenging because Gujarati and English do not translate directly. For example, the words used in English and Gujarati among elders versus those who are younger are different and essential to use accurately. In translation, she had to be careful when speaking to her parents so she didn't accidentally make the wrong translation from English. I could relate to Paru with this quite well because my language, Yoruba, also has certain words that do not translate accurately. In the Yoruba language, a single letter difference can change the meaning of a word to one with a different application. However, some of these words do not have a direct translation in English. This means there is a need to capture the nuances that result from using different combinations of English words. Paru explains, "Because my parents didn't speak much English, I have learned from experience to be very, very clear with exactly what I was saying, what my expectations were in any given sentence to ensure they understood it. Even now, when I say certain things to my dad, he mistranslates it, and he erupts, saying I'm being rude. And I'll have to make a distinction for him."

At thirty-one, Paru Radia immigrated to the United States. The change now becomes slight variations between British to American English. However, she has enough experience with the translation process to guide her work. She currently coaches executives to communicate clearly in order to get their desired results. Paru describes the irony of applying the skills that she has to use every day to help others do a better job of articulating their thoughts or requests especially at work. "In communication in general, I've always had to be so particular about my choice of language and my choice of words, to be understood."

In her current career as a coach, Paru can listen better to her clients and provide guidance because she has a broader viewpoint. She constantly coaches her executive clients on miscommunication awareness. It is important not to race to react but to instead pause and ask questions to confirm an understanding.

VOCAL TONE IN COMMUNICATION

Unlike verbal communication, other dimensions of communication barriers such as tone of voice can be more challenging to recognize. Carola Nitz, who immigrated from Berlin, Germany, felt confident in her English-speaking skills. The dominant language in Berlin is English. In addition, she also took part in an exchange program online while in Germany that was in partnership with an American university. After completing her engineering degree in Germany, she got a few years of work experience in Germany, and then she got her dream job in the US with Apple.

As an engineer, she discovered that although the ability to speak the English language wasn't a problem, her coworkers were getting offended by her tone. In Germany, the speaking style was more direct than on the US West Coast where she was located. Her statements would offend people.

"If you've done this shitty project, in Germany, someone else can say this project is shit. But they don't mean that in the sense that you personally suck at doing a project. It is more like, 'Here's why I think this is not working the way it works,' like let's move on and fix the problem."

The differences in how this is communicated in the United States compared to German was something Carola had to learn and apply because it impacted the way people perceived her as a person. She received comments that translated for her as, "You got to be a little bit nicer around here." As an engineer, Carola brought insights that were assets to the product design for a global market. However, the value of that unique perspective would not be realized if the team did not see beyond her communication differences. It is important to have a supportive team who can understand and tolerate the differences, leaving the space for learning and appreciation of unique values. In her next role, Carola was fortunate to have a supportive manager and team who highlighted the areas where the differences might cause misunderstanding. On the strength side, because she grew up in an environment where direct feedback was prioritized, Carola was very comfortable with receiving this feedback and adjusting.

For immigrants at work, it is important to recognize and accept that communication differences exist. This could be a disadvantage, but it can also be turned into an advantage. Many people would be more understanding if they knew that English is not the speaker's first language. In most cases at work, communication occurs so quickly that the interpretation is also quick and leaves no room to ensure it's been understood. Having the support in the workplace of people who understands that your cultural background is different from what they're used to can go a long way to help build confidence and create space for development. If you have an ally who understands that your cultural background is different from what they're used to, you can get more support as you integrate. Carola found that support and allyship with her manager, and that really helped her as she got settled in her corporate role in a new country.

One of my interviewees, whom I will refer to as "Helen," was born and raised in Bosnia and faced a similar challenge with communication tone. Her verbal tone came from her European background, and she was direct in her speaking style. Before starting her job at an American company in Bosnia, Helen only spoke her native Slavic language, named Bosnian. She had coworkers from the US and interacted with other locations; therefore, over the first few years, she taught herself how to speak, read, and write in English. When she got an opportunity to take up a different role with the company and relocate to the US office, she took it. Now, Helen found herself in a different environment where English was the dominant language. The translation from Bosnian to English was challenging, and she found it difficult to find the right words to express herself. More importantly, she got the feedback that her tone and communication came off strong, and she was perceived as rude. Helen said, "I'm very direct. I say how I mean it, not thinking about if I hurt your feelings, I was just focused on what needed to get done." It was not her intent to be rude, and she was not thinking in terms of feelings in these work-related scenarios.

A few months after Helen started at the US location, she started working on a project with a person who just seemed to dislike her and was not hiding it. "It just seemed this person could not stand my presence. It was to a point that it got me in tears a few times." The situation was baffling and uncomfortable for her, and a few months into the role, she decided to confront the coworker. To Helen's surprise, the feedback was about feelings and interpretations of her words that were not true at all. The coworker shared her resentment for the "rude" tone and all the constant "questioning" of her work. This all came as a surprise to Helen. "I asked a lot of questions to understand the process and make sure that what I was doing was correct. The intent was not to question my coworker's competence but to understand so I can better provide support." Once they both had a conversation over the differences in translation, they were able to have a productive outcome from the conversation. They became very good friends, communicated better, and became more culturally sensitive to their global coworkers.

Both Carola Nitz and Helen had a similar cultural background and received the same feedback on communication at work. The direct style of speaking was not a problem in their home country; it was understood and appreciated there. Working in the United States, these posed a major challenge. Fortunately, they were able to get helpful feedback that helped make changes to better achieve their communication intent. As Helen reflected on her twenty years of experience in corporate America, she acknowledged the changes she has had to make. "I have learned to soften my language. I had to find ways to get my point of view across without being perceived as rude."

WRITTEN COMMUNICATION

Another type of communication well used at work is email communication. For immigrants, using emails to communicate might be the easiest one to lean into as a default, mostly because we have a chance to edit and revise our words before we send them out. However, it is still possible to communicate the wrong message via email format. Lola Ajigbotafe's experience highlights a key example here.

An immigrant from Nigeria, Ajigbotafe was raised in a large Nigerian community in California. Growing up was a double nationality immersion experience for her. Her parents took extra care to make sure she was "Nigerian," and the entire Nigerian community was focused on passing the cultural values to the children. "I really felt like I got a strong sense of both worlds; I felt strongly Nigerian and I was American." As a Nigerian, one of those values was always being presentable. The expectation was always to present yourself appropriately in the context of your environment. Being presentable meant dressing appropriately when she left the house as a young girl. However, when she started work, being presentable also translated to interactions and communications style.

In email communications with coworkers, Ajigbotafe always stayed focused on the purpose of the email and went directly to the ask. She didn't engage in what she deemed unprofessional language, such as social questions, in her emails.

"I didn't say things like, 'Oh, hello, hope you're having a good day as well.' I didn't apply greetings, saying things like 'happy Friday.' I would just be black and white. I need A, B, and C."

From Ajigbotafe's perspective, getting right to the point in an email was professional. She saw adding on anything unnecessary to email communication as an unprofessional practice. When she took up a virtual role, Ajigbotafe had to use more email communications to get her work done. She did not get to have in-person connections with her new coworkers for a long time. This was not a problem for her as she felt that keeping her coworkers in a professional space was easily achieved. "I did not see a need for a lot of personal interactions." When she finally got an opportunity to interact in person with her new coworkers, Ajigbotafe was surprised at some of the feedback she received: "The way you come across in your emails—it's just so rude." Others sounded surprised to find out she was relatable: "Wow, you're so cool. I didn't know that. You're always so formal in your emails, but I didn't know you were cool."

Ajigbotafe's experience highlights something many of us might miss. Written conversations have a tone in addition to the message carried. As immigrants with a different first language, we can find that it is easier to default to written communication. While this is one of the essential formats at work, we can also unintentionally convey the wrong message. It is important to use different formats to communicate and to give others additional insights into who we are. Sometimes that might involve understanding the culture and the way other people like to receive communication or making changes to the way we word our emails. Since her intent was not to be cold or rude, Ajigbotafe was able to take the feedback and improve her emails to build relationships with her coworkers. She learned to draft written conversations that communicated warmth and helped bridge connections at work. As Lola Ajigbotafe concluded, "I had to learn that there is a tone in emails, there is a perceived tone, and I needed to be intentional about how I worded the messages to leave the impression I wanted."

DUAL LANGUAGE ADVANTAGE

"So often in life, things that you regard as an impediment turn out to be great good fortune."

—RUTH BADER GINSBURG

Communication is more often first seen as a barrier when you have a different first language. However, it can also be an advantage to have different languages in the workplace. Apart from being able to communicate with clients or customers from a different region with the same language, the process we eventually adopt to process the languages can add value to the quality of our work.

For Marielle Atanacio, an immigrant from the Philippines, creative expression is a significant aspect of her work as an art director. Marielle was born in the Philippines, and her family immigrated to the US when she was five. Her first language is Tagalog, and this remains the dominant language in communications with her family.

In the workplace, Marielle describes the challenges she faced as a creative professional attempting to express herself clearly and confidently at work. Knowing the expressions in one language and attempting to express that same creativity in a different language can be quite frustrating. "I might feel something, but I can't always say it as easily as some of my non-immigrant colleagues. They can just walk in a room and say exactly what they're feeling, and I get it."

Although these initially created challenges at work, she ultimately had to learn to leverage both her languages by bringing different perspectives together into one. Because of the complexities of thinking in two languages, she had to learn to think and prepare ahead of time so she was ready when it was time to give her input.

"Sometimes I have notes, or sometimes I talk to my mom or my brother. I ask, 'How do you explain this to someone? How do you know?' I ask if someone else has had to explain it. I still use my family."

Depending on the line of work, knowing two languages and having to spend some more time thinking between the two can mean leaning into two different perspectives in our own minds. That is an advantage that can help us do better work.

When we accept this and lean into it, we get to leverage a unique value and perspective to deliver better results.

That approach worked well in formal presentations or discussions, where providing input was critical for work to proceed. It might not work as well in the day-to-day conversations and engagements in the workplace. Marielle Atanacio realized she still needed to relieve that pressure on herself in daily engagements with her team. She used the term "conversations" when communicating casually and within spaces where she didn't get to prepare but still had to communicate especially with her teams.

THRIVING IN INTERSECTIONALITY WITH COMMUNICATION

As an immigrant, I might speak a little differently in one language, but I do speak and think in multiple languages. That's a communication advantage.

According to the US Census data, although English is the dominant language in America, more than 20 percent of US households do not speak English as their first language. Looking at the workplace specifically, according to the globalization partners annual survey, a large percentage of employees work on at least one global team, with communication challenges consistently emerging as one of the biggest challenges for work teams and leaders. This means for an immigrant coming into the US and in the workplace, the language barrier is just one aspect of the overarching communication barrier to deal with. We have multiple channels of communication and multiple interactions to evaluate, but we are not alone. It starts with awareness, but we also need to move to actions that can build better communications. How can we get better at communicating in the workplace as immigrants?

Speaking more, not less, is the key to getting better at speaking and building the needed confidence.

CHAPTER HIGHLIGHTS
- Pay attention: What is the preferred format of communication within my organization culturally?
- Pay attention: What is the geographical representation of my audience?
- Ask the audience: What is your preferred method of communication?
- Ask the audience: manager/team for feedback on communication deliverables (presentations, group emails, etc.).
- Explore: How can I get creative in leveraging my cultural background to communicate with others?
- Leverage resources: Email review tools, spell-check tools, communication programs, and master classes.

"We cling to hierarchies because our place in a hierarchy is, rightly or wrongly, a major indicator of our social worth."

—HAROLD J. LEAVITT.

CHAPTER SIX

HIERARCHY

———

INTRODUCTION

I grew up as part of a large extended family. My dad was the first of nine, and I grew up as the first of six children. In the Nigerian cultural setting, leadership expectations are conferred by virtue of your position in the family. The first-born child is the leader. Not every first-born child truly lives up to this expectation, but my dad lived up to it well. He was passionate about and responsible toward his siblings and extended family. He was also an engaged part of the academic community and the social network of the town in which I grew up. This meant I had an opportunity from a young age to observe him taking on and executing leadership. He always took a personal interest in the people around him and served as a mentor to students and my friends. His leadership always starts with listening, engaging, and connecting with people first.

The first time I was assigned to lead a large project in the US was an experience I had outside of my day job. Although I was employed in a large corporation as an individual contributor,

I led this project as part of a nonprofit organization I was involved with as a volunteer. I felt very unqualified because everyone on the team looked older in age than me. Since they were older, I also felt they should have more experience than I did, and it was intimidating to be given the responsibility to take charge of the project. However, I was able to focus on making myself available to get to know each team member. I provided a framework but also created an opportunity for everyone to have a say in the matter. I was under a lot of pressure but leaned into the leadership example I saw modeled as a child with Dad. Connecting with the people and building a relationship helped to successfully collaborate on the project, discover the team's unique strengths, and work together on a successful project. I am grateful for my dad's example and the volunteering opportunities outside of the workplace because these prepared me for leading in the corporate workplace.

HIERARCHY AND IMPACT ON LEADERSHIP STYLE

Yewande Shofela grew up in Nigeria as the first of four children. As the big sister to three boys, the responsibility to set the standards for her siblings motivated her growing up. She wanted to be able to provide any support needed for her brothers and excel in her career. Before she immigrated to the United States, she obtained her bachelor's degree and worked for eight years in the banking industry, where she had advanced to a supervisory position.

Her first job in the US was with a large biotechnology company. One of the first things she noticed was having to call employees who seemed old enough to be her parents by their first name, which was a culture shock and a bit uncomfortable for her. Observing everyone and accepting this as the norm, she was able to adapt. However, calling an older person by his or her first name didn't diminish the feeling of respect and recognition of authority. She always felt she had to defer when speaking or providing input at work.

"It was a little bit of inner frustration to me because I felt like I could not express myself enough. I didn't want to offend people or be disrespectful and had to watch my words with older colleagues."

As an individual contributor for the first few years, it was a little easier to adjust to the environment with a mix of generations at work. Yewande focused her effort on delivering high-quality results with her work within the financial space. Because she grew up leading by example to her younger siblings, she has always held herself to a higher standard by performing beyond expected standards at work. As an employee in the financial sector, this quality paid off and has guided her to success. "I think about how it happened, what I could have done better, and a personal assessment of the situation helps me to be more detailed and focused. These skills, coupled with my knowledge of the job and the desire to always wanting to take on more responsibilities, have been factors for my growth in the corporate space."

After a couple of years, there were some changes in her organization, and she got assigned another employee to support her. Moving from an individual contributor role to a manager role was challenging as she had high expectations. She was not part of the employee selection process of her direct report, which probably could have helped to determine their capabilities. It was challenging having to do a lot more training than anticipated and not getting the desired work output from the person.

"I was just spending so much time training, and I was really frustrated. If this person has a senior title, I expected that they should know certain things and I was not happy spending too much time teaching little details."

While being meticulous made her successful at her job, Yewande had a challenge when she was assigned an employee that didn't perform at the level she expected based on his title as a senior. It took a couple of months of feeling frustrated and stuck with multiple pieces of training. When she mentioned this to her manager, she also felt like she was not supported. "Eventually I realized I had set high expectations on his performance based on his title and my standards."

As Yewande learned, having the title did not indicate a high level of experience and competence in certain tasks. As a people manager, she had to learn to be patient and provide sufficient training while understanding that people learn at different rates. Having the right expectation at the beginning could have saved her time, lessened her frustration, and helped her get some support for her work much sooner. The key is to learn to assess individuals' skills and competency on an individual level regardless of the title to create a better hiring experience and onboarding.

"In the network model, rewards come by empowering others, not by climbing over them. If you work in a hierarchy, you may not want to climb to its top."

—JOHN NAISBITT

HIERARCHY AND BARRIER TO INTERACTION

The response to hierarchical cultural structures can be expressed in different ways depending on the country of origin. For Kwan Segal, her background determined how she conducted herself starting from her job search process. Kwan was born and raised in Bangkok, Thailand. She relocated to the United States with prior job experience in 2014 after a couple of visits to the United States for work and vacation. She had obtained her MBA online from a US institution, and with more than ten years of prior work experience, she didn't expect it to be difficult to find a corporate job.

As she began her job search, networking was very challenging for her. "When I meet someone for the first time, I speak humbly and softly." At the many interviews she attended, she presented herself politely. "I'm from a very small country and now we are here in the US, you know, top leader, the world leader, right?" She was used to "keeping the distance." In Asian culture, she describes keeping the distance as being polite and respectful to someone else. The phrase "power distance" Kwan used is called something different in each culture and always alludes to how respectful interactions are expected to be conducted. In Asian culture, the "power distance" provides the normal guidance to behaviors and is a part of how she was raised. "The distance for us means being polite; in America it means you're not confident."

During interviews, Kwan also found it difficult to promote her own work and accomplishments. As an Asian, the practice she grew up with promoted collectivism versus individualism. "When you do good things, you don't have to really spread it out. You can do good things and feel good about it. We are taught to value our bushels, but we don't have to really boast about it." This means that when she presented her work at interviews, she hardly took credit for anything she had done in her previous roles. One of the types of feedback from an interview was the hiring managers were not convinced she had done any of the things she had on her resumé because she used the word "we" consistently.

After she eventually got a job, Kwan also observed the casual ease of interactions between employees across different levels. Having casual friendships with her bosses was not natural for her. "I saw my colleagues having interactions and conversation with their bosses in a very casual way. And I felt so uncomfortable; saying all the casual words with the bosses sounded like kind of a friendship level, but it's the American way." In Asian culture, it was seen as being nosy to ask personal questions of others, especially your leaders. The casual interactions at work, particularly between high-level leaders and the employees, were new and different for her. In America, conversations with a manager or leader at work that included the ask about the family was all different but got a new result that she ultimately found had its own advantages. In the last eight years, Kwan has had the opportunity to learn to adapt to working in America. Her emails have improved to have less formality when communicating with leaders, and she constantly builds new connections through networking. Her job now includes providing the resources for international students that are needed to get into corporate workplaces and perform their best work. Her goal is not to lose her identity, but because she works and lives in America, she has taken the opportunity to observe and make changes to create a blend that works to thrive at work. Learning to own her role and interact with clients and coworkers in a way that showed her competence took stepping out of her comfort zone. "It took time for me to adjust and understand, but I found my comfort space where I can still be from Thailand and polite but also engage my bosses in a casual and friendly way."

HIERARCHY AND WORK STYLE IMPACT

Although Kwan's experience came from growing up in Thailand and immigrating to the US as an adult, immigrant women who moved to the US as children can also experience the power of distance. For Nat Morgan, although she grew up in the US, she grew up in an immigrant community. Her family was originally from Thailand, and she was raised in a strict Asian household. The strongest Asian cultural influence on her was the power distance and how to respond with reference to authority figures. "With Asian cultures, there's a high authority distance. You respect people who are older or in a higher position; you don't question it. From a conservative, traditional, kind of culture where women don't speak up, you are expected to do as they say and not question things."

When Morgan started her first job out of college, she worked in human resources for an Asian-owned company. She was asked to do menial tasks at the company, and she did these all without complaint. "I was the one that got the tea for visitors. There was a point at the holiday party where I was even asked to watch the vice president's kid." At the time, she did not think she had any option, as the CEO role and title is one she saw as important and powerful. In her opinion, at the time, being asked to perform any level of task by the CEO of a company meant you had to obey without question. It did not occur to her at all to question the authority on what she was being asked. This perspective at work also meant that she didn't voice her opinions often as an early career professional. She was good at following instructions from individuals older and at a higher level than herself, without questioning them.

Confronting people and speaking up is not something that comes naturally to her. However, as she advanced as a human resource professional, she realized she needed to learn to speak up and bring her ideas to the table. In her roles as a human resource business partner, especially within the STEM industry, the business partners she supports are mostly older males. One of the ways she has adapted to thrive is to listen so she can learn and be well prepared ahead of time. "Someone else might be able to come in with guns blazing. For me, a lot of it is sitting back and trying to understand and learn before I'm making a recommendation." It wasn't easy for her to form her response and provide input in the moment, but she learned the value of doing her thinking and reflecting before entering the room.

With her cultural background and as someone more introverted, her role is intimidating to her. However, she loves what she does, and she knew she wanted to make a difference for the businesses she supports. Analyzing the data and preparing ahead of time gave her a lot of tools to approach her meetings, ready to provide meaningful insights. "By the time the recommendation is made, it's well thought out. It's all supported. And at the end of the day, I'm not here to push against people. I am bringing people together to understand that I'm here to help."

One of the strengths Morgan also has is her interest in getting to meet and connect with diverse people. Her childhood neighborhood in the Los Angeles County area was a mix of families from all over the world. Most of the neighborhood residents were also immigrants from different countries. The diversity of her neighborhood as a child was what sparked an interest in people and motivated her to pursue cultural studies in college. Her interest in human resources as a career path was a direct reflection of the cultural interactions she had experienced as a child. As Nat summarized, "The system that I've created for myself is to get to know the leaders on an individual basis so that I don't feel so personally uncomfortable questioning them."

Respecting people, their journeys, and individual experiences is important. As immigrants, we must learn to balance that with our individual opinions and insights to contribute in our own way without disrespect or having to change who we are. Depending on the roles we have, taking the time to get to know a person can help us do our job successfully without losing the individual perspective.

THRIVING IN INTERSECTIONALITY WITHIN A HIERARCHY
Every human deserves respect; every title does not.

In corporate organizational systems and structures, the leadership title is often weighted with huge responsibilities based on the title or the level. However, people get promoted in a role for different reasons, not just for their level of experience. To support, training sessions are made available. Ultimately, people always have an opportunity to grow into leading people both with technical and social skills. The missing aspect in promotions and the assignment of roles in corporate organizations is that it does not indicate a specific style or guarantee competence in leading. From my cultural experience as a Nigerian, I know there is the natural power distance and responsibility designation determined by age difference. It is easy to respect and follow an older person who is more experienced than you are and has a higher title. But this basic assumption that age and titles are directly related to wisdom, responsibility, and respect can set immigrants up with false expectations in the workplace.

CHAPTER HIGHLIGHTS

- The leader is not always right.
- Title confers power but does not determine the skillset.
- Set realistic expectations and not by the title.
- Our cultural backgrounds can also be an asset.
- Leaders can learn from subordinates and vice versa.

"It's not what you know or who you know but who knows you."

—SUSAN ROANE

CHAPTER SEVEN

COMMUNITY

INTRODUCTION

My childhood in Nigeria was a great example of the saying, "It takes a village to raise a child." Thousands of miles away, I still remember all the families I grew up around in the two different neighborhoods in which I was raised. Holidays, birthdays, graduations, and job announcements were shared and celebrated. In addition, on every major holiday, we would take dishes of food to our next-door neighbors and would receive some in return. Neighbors were family and could constantly drop by unannounced during the day. You have a dependable network of friends in your neighborhood as the first point of call if there is ever a need.

In contrast to how I grew up, my first work environment in corporate America was different. Although we sat in a shared workspace for several hours a day, we were all separated by padded high walls. My coworkers all had slightly different work hours and different roles. The most significant thing we sometimes shared was the space and a manager. We were closer through group emails for shared tasks rather than connecting in person, especially during work. It felt a little isolated and awkward to work together, spending so many hours with one another yet not knowing each other or having any conversations outside of work. Thinking about what type of work I enjoy, what organizations I want to work with, and my leadership style, I am always drawn to that feeling of community and seek to connect with people. It is not a right or a wrong way of leading. But it is a style that comes from how I grew up and has helped me be better at my corporate jobs at building connections.

BACKGROUND AND COMMUNITY

Tosin Musa understood this feeling of community. She was born and raised in Nigeria as the third of five kids. She described growing up with different members of her extended family living with them for months at a time. "At every point, we would usually have a minimum of fourteen people living under our roof." She got comfortable living with and getting to know different people and getting along with them. Before relocating to the United States, she earned her degree from a college half an hour from her house. She also worked for six years in the same city. She describes her work experience as similar to her home; her workplace was a community of connected employees. "I worked in an office with three other people, and we were like family. We all knew about each other's families and interacted as such. We regularly held discussions that were not work-related. That was just the way we worked together."

When she moved to the United States at age thirty-one, it was for a doctoral program. Although she had her husband

and young daughter with her, this was the smallest unit of a family she had ever had around her. In the four years she spent in graduate school, she was able to connect with other international students and immigrant families in the same doctoral program.

When she got her first corporate job after her doctorate program, it was in a different city and her family had to move. She naturally stepped in at work with the expectation of building a new community. In her workplace, she found out that the level of interaction was different. People interacted on a work basis, and communications were only concerning deliverables. "People just talked to you when they needed something from you. No one interacted or socialized in the mornings or during break times. It was very different from what I was used to and very lonely too."

Tosin observed people quietly walk in and step into their workspaces in the mornings. As the newest member of the team, she also conducted herself in this manner, but it was uncomfortable for her. She found it challenging to work in an environment for an extended time, while everyone was maintaining their distance. Coming into the department as the only immigrant and one of two Black people, she felt different. She wanted to connect and get to know her coworkers, but she saw her coworkers did not model this at work. She struggled to understand how things were done. After a while, Tosin decided to step outside the norm she observed. She intentionally approached everyone she encountered with a friendly smile. When Tosin met other employees, she made eye contact, smiled, and shared a verbal greeting. "Even if they were not responding, I chose to keep smiling and exchanging pleasantries with everyone I came across." The desire was strong for a community that she did not currently see.

In Musa's case, the background and culture she grew up with highlighted a challenge for her as she entered the workplace. Because of her cultural background, she came in with the expectation to naturally lean on her work network. She discovered it was different at her company. She made the decision to approach the situation in her natural expectation: by seeking a connection. Because of her background, interacting with everyone else was easier for her than keeping quiet. Across hierarchies and levels, she extended the same friendliness and social courtesy to every coworker. Her upbringing helped her successfully build connections at work and connect authentically with her coworkers. The connections and network gave her confidence in her new job. Gradually, she noticed that people gravitated toward her and began to respond to her. She built a network and developed the community at work. "Now I have a connected network. If there is information that I need, I know who to ask. I know who I am working with, and they feel like friends."

CONFIDENCE THROUGH COMMUNITY

Rekha Prodduturi, who was born and raised in India, came to the US with prior work experience. I introduced Rekha in chapter three from her experience with legal barriers. However, the legal barriers were not the only limitation she encountered. As an experienced professional who had worked in the same industry for a few years, Rekha had also done a lot of traveling and felt she was prepared to live in a different country and culture. However, it wasn't the culture shock that really stood out for her.

"Maybe it's just a perception and people often do not see you like that, but internally I was questioning if I was as good as other people. My confidence was shaken, and I found I was questioning my own abilities, which never happened when I worked in India."

Rekha was concerned if her homegrown skills would fit in the new work environment and even how her team and clients perceived her. The internal conversations and fears that she had were holding her back from delivering at her full potential in the first few months. She finally recognized that even if she had to do more than other people and do things differently, she did not want to lose her individuality and identity while learning. Growing up in India as part of a large family system, Rekha had experience in managing complex situations with people by listening and assessing the situation. "By nature, being a part of a joint family at home have helped a lot in terms of adaptability and seeking understanding." To apply those same skills at work, she needed to build her network. She found mentors and built relationships through networking. She learned to apply the skills she had as an immigrant woman to her advantage by being patient, observing, and then approaching her projects and work with caution and new rigor.

"Networking became the tool that I used to learn new skills and build my confidence. But it didn't come naturally. I started by making a conscious effort to approach and connect with new people every week both within and outside the company. Over the years, I have been successful in building a network of trusted friends and mentors, who not only valued my professional contributions but also helped me embraced my authenticity and cultural identity."

In her current role as a voice of the customer lead for Amazon Integration, Rekha gets to help elevate immigrant voices within the organization as a part of her formal role from both the customer and the employee perspectives. She creates forums and mechanisms to educate leaders within the company and external service partners on immigrant experiences and thus making an impact on immigration journeys for thousands of employees.

BARRIERS TO BUILDING COMMUNITY

The flip side of the cultural impact on workstyle is that it can also become barriers that need to be overcome to advance at work. Betty Huang, who was born in China and immigrated with her dad and stepmom at age eleven, was not surrounded by a large Asian community. Within her small family unit, her parents tried their best to raise her culturally by introducing traditional foods and speaking Chinese at home. Most importantly, her mom in China tried to incorporate the cultural values they were raised with even though they were a sea apart. One area was a focus on the practice of humility and hiding your accomplishments and competence. The mindset was that you are in competition with everyone, and you need to protect yourself and hide your work.

"In China, you don't show off or promote yourself too much because of the competition. The tendency is for everyone to work hard quietly and achieve success without self-promoting."

Huang went into the workplace with this mindset: keeping your head down, working hard toward your goal, and letting your final successful result speak for itself. This worked well for a while, and she built her career in sales. Huang found she worked best when she had control over achieving her individual goals. In her individual contributor sales role, individual members of the team had goals and targets. She successfully proved her competence by delivering excellent results.

"I just want to succeed quietly and show my numbers. I'm going to do my own thing quietly, and then you can see my results at the end."

Although succeeding as a sales professional has been primarily driven by working hard toward her individual goal, she realized that was not sustainable. At a certain stage of her career, she realized she needed help in certain areas. She needed a network of people to advance, and she didn't have any. In a professional setting, she was used to not having a network and working individually toward her goal. However, she needed to bring a different skill set into the workplace to thrive. Growing up in an environment where she didn't have a lot of people that looked like her and with a small family unit, she had a different skill set that she could leverage.

"Because I also have that advantage of understanding cultural differences, once I tried, I connect well with people from all different types of backgrounds. My friend circle now has every kind of person from everywhere."

She realized that being independent or ambitious can be a barrier, and there was still a need for community and a network of support as she sought to develop and advance in the workplace.

Although she had grown up skilled at building connections across diverse groups, she had never had to bring that into the workplace. She grew up believing the professional workplace needed an individualist work style. Once that barrier was identified, she was able to tap into her cultural background for a different skill set: building connections across cultures. She was able to build an internal network of people she could lean on when she needed support at work.

"Your network is your net worth."

—PORTER GALE

LEVERAGING COMMUNITY

Dr. Lola Awoniyi-Oteri was born in Nigeria and immigrated to the United States with her family at age nineteen to go to college. In the early part of her career, she struggled with being misunderstood, wrong perceptions, and receiving negative reviews that did not align with her actual performance. Coming from a background where people were direct and expressive, what she called passion was not welcomed in the workplace. "I struggled with expressing myself at work and a lot of my initial reviews indicated high ratings on technical contributions; I was perceived as being too brash, too aggressive, not approachable." To accommodate what she felt was expected, she tried to dial down on her emotions and engagement. Then the complaints shifted to insufficient engagement at work. "I wasn't being perceived the way

I thought I was presenting myself." The pressure of trying to maintain performing excellently at her job while managing people's perceptions was taking its toll.

Awoniyi-Oteri had a manager, who is currently still a mentor to her. This was the only female manager she had met in her career so far, and this leader had a lot of prior experience that she was able to share. "I observed she communicated in a pleasant and approachable manner. Even when she was engaging in controversial or difficult discussions, I noticed she brought some levity to the conversation, sometimes by laughing or smiling while still speaking her mind. It was hard for anyone to get angry with her." This manager/mentor also encouraged Awoniyi-Oteri to build a network of connections within the company and to get to know people so she could be seen as non-threatening in the workplace. As a natural introvert, making an effort to connect internally and build her network was not an easy process for her. "I had to learn to become a bit extroverted, to spend time socializing with coworkers and create an atmosphere where people get to know me and are comfortable with me."

"At some point I realized if I'm going to be myself and not misunderstood, I'm going to be positive, do my best in incorporating these learnings from my mentor, and take the pressure off."

She also engaged an external coach who helped her navigate the difficult stages when the issues were not necessarily anything she needed to change. In cases when she felt toxicity in the workplace or on the project, she had to stop taking on the blame. "The coach actually helped to break the cycle, the mentality of always putting things on myself."

It took her a while, but she discovered the power of building a community with peers and finding internal mentors. "At the end of the day, it took me a while to just slowly just find my balance, to get to a place where I can be myself and learn how to do that."

She didn't have these networks or understanding earlier on and went through a lot to find her support at work. "Now I have sponsors who believe in me. I have people who let me make my mistakes. They're not cutting you off or demanding a mold of presenting oneself but allowing me to contribute effectively in my own unique way."

There was a season when she didn't find that network internally, and she had to seek external opportunities. Volunteering for committees and external organizations helped show her work and develop her interpersonal skills, which also resulted in internal validation. "I was open to external opportunities, and this proved to be useful internally in the long run."

THRIVING IN INTERSECTIONALITY WITH COMMUNITY
As an immigrant in the workplace, it is essential to find your tribe.

Entering the US corporate world, I had not only moved thousands of miles from home but now also from the new home I had built in the first sixteen months while I was in graduate school. I certainly did not have a network when I started my first role. However, growing up like I did in a connected community, I knew the power of networks, and I craved that. I learned to build networking into my professional life through a supportive manager, internal organization mentors, and external volunteer projects. I have continued to leverage that to expand my connections in different spaces over the last eleven years. Internal organization committees and employee resource groups (ERGs) became a key part of my experience within the organizations I worked in. In the last few years, with globalization and hybrid work formats, workplaces have had to pay attention to how workers stay connected and engage with each other. Although we recognize that the interactions and community building are important parts of the culture for employees, having a physical setup does not mean that people want to interact socially in the workplace. As a member of an underrepresented group, the people's assumptions originated from multiple perspectives. However, by finding and connecting with a supportive few, there is a mutual benefit of learning while also educating others: helping people get to know our personalities and individualities.

As immigrants, the community we desire can look different depending on different factors such as industry, location, and stage of life. Because I grew up around gender inequities and a culture of pre-defined expectations for women, I desired to surround myself with women who were doing things I admired in the workplace. As my career progressed, I have had a need for different communities, and I continue to expand my circle as needed. For example, when I had my first child, I craved a community of working moms that season. I went beyond just looking for career women and female leaders to looking for moms who had found great ways to balance parenting and building careers. For immigrants at work, the environment can feel exclusive and lonely because that is what underrepresentation creates. However, all we need is a few others to connect and support our journey to belonging and authenticity at work. The community that the audience for this book can create for you is a one of immigrants in the professional space with resources and tips to support your journey.

CHAPTER HIGHLIGHTS

- There are different dimensions of diversity. Define what dimensions you feel the greatest need for support.
- Identify the unique perspective you have from your background and differentiate between barriers or strengths.
- Focus on communities that provide resources to help build on your strengths or remove cultural barriers.
- Identify the right individuals and organizations that can inspire your career.
- To connect with a community of immigrants in the corporate workplace, join the LinkedIn community "Thriving in Intersectionality—Immigrants in Corporate."

"When I was nine years old, *Star Trek* came on, I looked at it, and I went screaming through the house, 'Come here, Mum, everybody, come quick, come quick! There's a Black lady on television, and she ain't no maid!' I knew right then and there I could be anything I wanted to be."

—WHOOPI GOLDBERG

CHAPTER EIGHT

REPRESENTATION

———

INTRODUCTION

Sometime in my pre-teen years, I was sitting in the living room in my home in Nigeria with the TV on. I was not really paying attention to the TV until an image came on that drew my attention. It was an interview with a female bank executive. I don't specifically remember the context of the interview or even the woman's name. What stood out for me was the way she was dressed and the way she spoke. She was dressed formally in a pantsuit, poised, well-articulated, and showing so much confidence. It wasn't an image I was familiar with for women around me. She sounded like she really knew what she was talking about, and the interviewer, a male, was listening to her every word. I remember thinking I wanted to be just like her when I grew up.

I didn't know what a corporate career meant at the time. But I have remembered enough about that image on a television screen as I have moved through my career. The vision of what I could be even as a woman has stayed with me. There is power in setting goals, but this is further imprinted when we have a visual image attached to it. I held unto the vision without a clear path. I wasn't one of the kids that knew the exact career they wanted to pursue. But, when I had the opportunity for an internship for four weeks at a construction company, I was excited to take it. When I had one for a six-month internship, I knew what general area I wanted to explore. I was drawn to the type of spaces that took me closer to what I envisioned every day. And in each of these spaces I always found a mentor, someone who had been where I wanted to be, and I stayed close enough to learn and gain some guidance.

"A lot of people have gone further than they thought they could because someone else thought they could."

—ZIG ZIGLAR

IDENTITY AND MISSING REPRESENTATION

For Anu Iwanefun, who was introduced in chapter two, she was born in Nigeria, and the feeling of sticking out, struggling to identify the Black American identity, and recognizing a lack of representation has only grown deeper as she moved from college to corporate America. Anu immigrated after her high school education in Nigeria at the age of sixteen. Her college experiences were in Indianapolis and Tennessee before starting work in Chicago. In college, she heard different references about being Black from her Black American friend, and it was a new concept for her, identifying based on her skin color. It was confusing and with a depth that she couldn't understand.

"I didn't grow up struggling with things because I'm Black. I was like, 'What does that really mean?'"

Although she confidently identified as an immigrant woman, she felt as if she was missing an identity that she didn't understand. She signed up for African American and African Studies because she wanted to learn more. "I think I had to take these classes on African American history because I realized that being in this country, I'm going to be classified as Black."

After obtaining her master's degree in public health, she got her first job at the University of Chicago cancer research clinic, and her first boss was a well-renowned Nigerian doctor. "Seeing a Nigerian woman heading the clinic was very inspiring to me. She was very smart, and I learned so much from her. I learned about clinical research; it piqued my interest and guided my career."

When Anu met her husband and moved to San Diego, she got into the biotechnology industry field. The lack of gender and ethnic diversity was apparent. She missed having people she could relate to and felt like she had to shrink herself to adapt to the workplace.

"My biggest struggle was not having any Black women immigrants or Black women in authority, no one rooting for me, no one pushing for me, advocating for, or supporting me. It felt like I just had to figure it out for myself."

Anu always remembers her first boss who looked just like her and inspired her to pursue her dreams. The struggle to keep embracing her identity and find representation to motivate her work has been a constant part of her career journey. In her current industry, it is more difficult to find the representation she seeks to inspire her. However, she has learned to leverage external organizations to find mentors who look like her or have a similar background and leadership roles in STEM.

Now she realizes more can be done in attracting diverse talent like her into STEM and the clinical affairs field. In her current position, where she gets to hire and influence decisions on hiring, she is actively advocating for diversity and representation. As a hiring manager in STEM, she seeks to help minorities embrace their identities and find the representation they need. She also encourages managers to think inclusively during recruitment efforts. As Anu summarizes, "The doors were open for me. Now I always ask, 'How do I now open more doors for other people? How do I let people and especially minorities know what career choices are possible in the clinical affairs space and in STEM?'"

IDENTITY AND FINDING MENTORS

Although Khue Tran immigrated at a young age, she grew up in a neighborhood where she didn't see many people who looked like her. Khue was born in Vietnam. When she was six years old, she immigrated to the United States with her family, and they settled in Boca Raton, Florida. The town and neighborhood had a large population of retired white residents. This meant that, unlike most Asian immigrants, they didn't have a large Asian community around. She didn't have many cultural connections as a child. "I was always having this identity battle, like, I'm Asian but I'm not Asian enough but I'm also not white enough to be white. I really couldn't figure out who I am and where I belonged." Khue went through several years in elementary school without meeting anyone from her cultural background or who looked like her, until she met one other Asian girl in fifth grade. "When I first saw her, I was like, 'Oh my God—you look like me. That's crazy.' So, we hit it off and became best friends. We went to middle school and high school together, and she is still my best friend to this day."

Even when she went on to meet other Asians in high school, she never really connected. There was always the consciousness of standing out and being different from the majority. Everyone else always had a different experience or background, and she was not fitting in.

"I had a high school friend tell me that I wasn't Asian enough to be in their group. I didn't belong with the Asians, and I didn't really belong with any other groups, so I just never really had a ton of friends. And then in college I didn't connect with any group."

Grappling with these identity questions, Khue kept her head down and did the bare minimum, especially with tasks and school. This impacted her ability to figure out her career path and what she wanted to do with her life. Although she didn't have a clear career path, at the end of her college degree, she was fortunate to get an internship after her science undergrad degree that got converted to a full-time position. Her plan was just to get her feet wet and figure out what the next steps might be for her; she didn't really have any grand career ideas. She eventually started to seek mentors and, based on several conversations, got moved to a role within the finance team. "I was working in finance, reporting directly to the VP of finance and a CFO/COO. Both became my mentors and advocates. They both really saw potential in me and encouraged me to push beyond what I thought I was capable of. I feel lucky to have had such amazing mentors here because sometimes all it takes is for someone to see you."

In addition, as an immigrant and only child, and with all the identity questions, Khue was a little isolated as a child and started off in corporate with a hard-working and individualistic mindset.

"I was very shy to speak up. I thought I just had to keep my head down and to follow the rules. This meant not asking for raises, promotions, or seeking new positions. But if you keep your head down and work, no one's going to know that you're unhappy doing what you're doing. They don't know that you want to do more. Speaking up and asking for more is so important. By doing so, I was able to have seven roles and promotions in just under seven years."

For someone who didn't have a clear career path or drive at the beginning, it took a mentor and a great manager to see the potential and get her thinking in the direction of going back to school. Khue never intended to go back to school until she began speaking with her mentors. She ended up going back and getting an MBA degree. Once she discovered the power of mentoring, Khue continued to take advantage of that. She continues to seek representation for what she wants and finds people willing to guide and mentor her. She actively reached out to leaders in positions and with projects that she gets to shadow and opportunities to take advantage of. Representation for her didn't necessarily look like her, but she got comfortable reaching out to find leaders who believed in her and motivated her even when they didn't look like her.

"I learn to reach out to different people with various backgrounds and experiences because having different perspectives and finding the right mentor chemistry is important. Not all of them are going to say yes or they're not all going to be a good match. It's critical to learn from someone who has done it before who can guide you to make the right decisions. My mentors today have really changed my life and continue to provide me with resources to be successful."

LEVERAGING EXTERNAL NETWORKS

Dr. Lola Awoniyi-Oteri, who was introduced in chapter seven for her experience leveraging community, was also strongly impacted by representation. She started in Atlanta and eventually graduated from Stanford with her doctorate in electrical engineering. As an undergraduate, she was fortunate that she was in the United States at a time when international students were able to apply for internships as undergraduates.

When Awoniyi-Oteri was at Georgia Tech, there was an alumnus from Georgia Tech who was currently a leader at a leading semiconductor company and came back on an outreach effort to recruit minority interns. She went through the application process and was selected for the internship program. "Even though I had a high GPA, I would not have had that opportunity as an international student looking for internships. As a minority and an alumnus, this leader came back and was looking for minorities in the engineering program with high GPAs."

That summer, she got a lot of technical knowledge and hands-on experience in her engineering field. Prior to the internship, her goal had been to get her master's and maybe go back home to Nigeria. "I attended a meeting of Black PhDs in a leading semiconductor company and met several Black male PhDs, most of whom graduated from MIT. They now worked at this reputable company, conducting research, developing innovative ideas, and having a significant impact in the field." She had never thought about getting a PhD until she attended that meeting. Looking at all these high-ranking leaders and what they were doing at the company, what they had created, and the technology they were working on, she started thinking for the first time that summer that she really needed to think seriously about a PhD if she were to achieve the type of success she desired in her field. "If I didn't see that group, I wouldn't have been inspired to explore a doctorate program."

Awoniyi-Oteri didn't have many women in her field, neither Black nor white, so she was used to being the only one. The large representation of Black men was a seed of possibilities, and she went on to apply for and complete her PhD program. The internship also gave her an existing network to reach out to after college. On a student visa status, there were limited opportunities with companies that were able to sponsor work visas. Because she was already in the company network and had a prior history, she got priority when she applied for a full-time job. "I got that internship because someone gave me a chance. If I didn't get that internship, I wouldn't have been exposed to career opportunities in research and development early in my educational journey. This exposure has allowed me to pursue a career path that has enabled me to make significant contributions to my field including authoring over 300 worldwide patents and patent applications."

"Mentoring is a brain to pick, an ear to listen, and a push in the right direction."

—JOHN C. CROSBY

CREATING REPRESENTATION

Sandhya Jain-Patel, an Indian immigrant, observed her dad, a corporate employee, when she was growing up. She can say the lessons from him were applicable regarding how one should dress, speak, and behave. He had always been a strong representative role model for her; however, stepping into the corporate workplace Sandhya realized there was so much more to learn.

"I don't know how to sign an email, how to answer the phone, how to be in a meeting. While that may not be American culture, that may be corporate culture to an extent, but I think just even knowing that there is a difference, knowing that there should be an approach when you are in corporate space is very important." When entering a new environment, it's helpful to have all the options in front of you and to pay attention to them. You can't copy or be someone else and do it justice. Sandhya's first boss was a white European male. "I knew that I couldn't model my behavior after my white, European male boss, right? Because no one is going to receive what I say the same way he says it." She had to find a model at a different level of someone to learn from. It was important for her to know all the available options in the first few years of work.

For Sandhya, her first represented group was women, which was first about the gender. She looked for different women she respected and who were willing to role model for her. Then when she became a mom, she realized she needed a different type of representation and model. "Before I went on maternity leave, I took every single mother at Christie's New York out to coffee, to just find out like what that experience was like, pre- and post-maternity."

For immigrant women to get in and advance in corporate America, representation is important. Sandhya recognized the need for women to understand that, and the path she had to go herself eventually led to her building her own group of people. Based on different skills, visions, and goals, she identified individuals she admired and connected with. "I wanted to find the people who resonate with me authentically, whether it's in value or experience or they just look like me in some way."

Sandhya was at her company for almost ten years before she had enough data and information to start an employee resource group—a group within the organization of women who served as a network for motivating each other and sharing resources and skills. Women who were just like her were looking for ways to grow and thrive at work. As she describes, "You want people to go away from meeting you and say your name to other people, right? So that's what I created there. A network of women that supported each other. I couldn't have done that my first couple years. You must really understand what there isn't and what is missing before you can take that step."

LEVERAGING ALLIES

Sofia Bennet-Hymas was born in Mexico. As the only girl in her family, her mother sent her to an English school in order to give her the best opportunities in life. "My mother was convinced that if I learned another language, I was going to have better chances in life, and she was right." Sofia was able to complete her education in human resources and was working in Mexico with an American company. She did not have plans to immigrate until she met her husband at a work conference in New York. He didn't speak any Spanish, so it was easier for her to immigrate to join him in her late twenties. When Sophia's company found out she was planning to immigrate, they offered her a different role based out of New York. She was able to stay with the same company and get a promotion getting off to a good start in a new environment. Although she was familiar with the vibrance and cultural diversity of New York from her visits for work, their home was two hours north of New York City. The city where they lived and commuted to work from was not diverse. In addition to home environment adjustment, she was now also a minority at work, as most of her new colleagues were American-born.

Although she had already worked for the same company before immigrating and she did speak English, it was still a surprisingly different experience living among employees whose primary language was English. She found a need to pay closer attention at work meetings to follow along because people spoke too quickly. "The big learning curve steps for me was waiting to be given a voice as an employee. I didn't make a lot of contributions because I waited to be called on."

A few months into the role, Sofia was in a meeting at work. At one point, they said something that she understood well and had a strong opinion about because she had the experience from one of the countries they were discussing: Mexico. "I raised my hand and then my boss at the time, of a perfectly white Irish background, turned and called on me. I explained what my position was and shared my thoughts." The conversation resumed, and after a few more deliberations, her boss turned toward her and said, "Sofia, I think you will be the best person to lead this project." This was a shock to her and not something she was used to. Her role was an individual contributor role; back in Mexico, in a similar role, the projects were given mostly to men, the boss, or somebody higher up. Sofia completed the project successfully and will always remember the chance the manager gave her, especially with her being new and without an established network in the United States. "As I continued to establish my voice and grow my career, I realized the value of finding people who understood and saw me and willing to give me an opportunity."

Sofia had the experience and the qualifications. However, cultural barriers and language challenges caused her to hold back at work. It took finding someone who heard her and saw the perspectives she brought as valuable enough to give her an opportunity to take the lead on an important project.

Another experience she had with an important mentor was in the season after having her twins. As a new parent, Sofia was struggling to juggle everything and didn't feel like her new manager empathized or had anything in common with her. A different manager, a Puerto Rican woman who was also a mother, saw the struggles she was having with her role and the visible lack of support from her manager. "She's like, 'Come work for me. I understood where you are and what you are going through. I have a job that will be perfect for you, but it will be a demotion, so think about it.'"

Sofia accepted that offer and ended up working her way up to a promotion the next year. She never regretted making a move that season and always remembered the leader who saw her, connected with her, and gave her an opportunity. In Mexico, she was used to building and leveraging personal relationships. She didn't have that in the United States, but she learned that in corporate America as an immigrant, you can build the right professional relationships and get the support that you need to get your work done.

THRIVING IN INTERSECTIONALITY WITH REPRESENTATION

The representation we see builds our confidence so we are ready to be the representation we don't see.

Strong representation can show up at different stages and impact the trajectory of our careers. For me, it started before I got into corporate America; for Dr. Lola Awoniyi-Oteri, it was during her internship program. For Anu Iwane-fun, Khue Tran, and Sandhya Jain-Patel, representation and the career impact that came with it occurred while at work in corporate America. As an immigrant entering a global corporate environment, depending on the industry, diversity, and representation can look different, but the impact can be critical to helping to pull through difficult seasons and against barriers at work. Finding a community or individuals who see the potential and are willing to take steps to help build our career can make a big difference. A key part of my inspiration for writing this book is for immigrant women to find that community with other immigrant women who have been in similar situations and develop insight from their experiences. It is impactful when the right representation is seen, and the right mentors, sponsors, and champions go that extra mile to inspire and motivate others.

I have realized in my corporate career that not everyone will be supportive. But sometimes, we find the right ally, champion, advocate, mentor, or sponsor in the most unexpected places, and we realize a few are just enough.

CHAPTER HIGHLIGHTS
- Owning your cultural identity in the workplace is not easy, but it is essential in order to find the people who will embrace and support your authenticity journey.
- Identify leaders or peers who have some underrepresented intersections and learn from their journey.
- Determine what missing representation is important to you and go after building connections in the groups.
- Stretch out of your comfort zone and build relationships with people unlike you.

- Do not be limited to your current company, industry, or role in the search for mentors.
- Look for opportunities that might look unrelated to your role but can lead to long-term support.

"When a workplace becomes toxic,
its poison spreads beyond its walls and into
the lives of its workers and
their families."

-—GARY CHAPMAN

CHAPTER NINE

TOXIC WORKPLACES

———

INTRODUCTION

I came to the United States as a student, but the route into the academic space as an international student is definitely a different experience than the corporate workplace. I was excited because, of course, coming into the United States of America with any type of visa is a great opportunity. The excitement of moving into a country where the services and amenities were more dependable than in my home country was not something I took for granted. I came from a background where community, connections, and relationships were important and part of my life, but the education systems and career options were not as clear, especially with the high population in Nigeria. As I made admission plans, course registration, travel plans, and living arrangements remotely, I was continuously impressed by the process and support available even from a distance. I worked directly with the international student office to make my living arrangements and had a map of where my apartment was and the distance to my classes. I arranged for the campus shuttle to pick me up upon arrival and got the details for the nearest stores and what items I really needed to bring or not. The support I had from the international students' office teams, student advisors, and all the departments I had contact with went a long way to make the transition easier. Once I arrived, I met other international students from different parts of the world, and we were supported in settling in so we could focus on our classes. Yes, this is a country where processes are in place, and it worked. I got into the country, started my program, and got plugged in on campus almost immediately.

However, the academic system and support for international students' entry vary by institution and is different from the corporate workplace. The graduate school experience in my case was for sixteen months, I finished earlier than planned, and I realized why most people take their time in college, especially on a student visa. The process of transitioning from college into the corporate workplace does not work that smoothly, even if you do not have the legal limitations. The networks and resources specially created in graduate school set the expectations that the corporate workplace works the same way, but the two are not the same. As I started in corporate America, carrying over my experience getting into school and the support I received, I still really believed that the systems and support were in place for me at work. But I found out nothing was really designed to uniquely support me as an immigrant applicant or employee. The right institution and workplaces matter, but it is not always easy to recognize the difference. As immigrants, even when we end up in toxic workplaces, we end up internalizing a lot of behaviors directed at us.

FINDING YOUR VOICE

One of my interviewees, whom I will call "Priya," was born and raised in India. Growing up in a culture where male and female children do not always get the same opportunities for education, her father made sure Priya and her brother had all the same opportunities and were able to make decisions for themselves. "I was always raised to be independent, not to rely on people too much." After her undergraduate degree, she decided to immigrate to the United States for better career opportunities. Priya had a strong Indian community in graduate school, and the challenges were minimized. Her first job after school was as a senior research technician job in a lab, and it was an environment where she was a target for toxic actions.

In the lab, each employee had their designated workspace, and everyone was expected to clean up after themselves. However, a colleague would leave the cleanup work to Priya. Since this had to be done each day and he left earlier, she did not feel she had a choice but to do the cleanups. She also had a colleague who made inappropriate sexual comments at work. Seeing as she was an immigrant and this was her first job, she was not sure of what actions to take. "I had no idea that I have a place and a system in place where I can go and complain about people with inappropriate behaviors." Although her employer did have legal protections for employees at work and there was a process to report inappropriate behaviors, this was not something she was familiar with or aware of.

For all employees, particularly an immigrant new to the system, employee protection policies shouldn't be difficult to determine or leverage. Either through ignorant acts or intentional acts of microaggressions, employees can conduct themselves inappropriately toward immigrants. Priya describes a situation in which a coworker at the senior level made a comment in the lab about immigrants that he presented as a compliment: "This international technician that I had, she never says no to work on weekends or late hours. Americans always need weekends and make too many requests—too much drama." For Priya, when she heard the comment, she knew what he meant. She did the same thing saying yes to extra work, but it wasn't because she wanted to do it. "I took on more work than I could handle because I was always worried about saying no even when I do not have the capacity." As an immigrant that came in through a student visa, Priya's legal stay in the United States was dependent on the right job related to her degree and a corresponding sponsor company. Although the conditions at work were not ideal, she didn't feel like she was in any situation to complain. "I was not going to do anything to jeopardize my legal status and lose my job."

As an immigrant raised to be independent, she got comfortable doing things by herself and did not have a network at work. Priya took independence to mean she needed to figure it all out by herself and struggled with the reality of her work environment, feeling unequipped to handle it. The fear of speaking up held her back and kept her mentally exhausted for a long time. "Speaking up, I knew two things can happen, either getting fired or some discrimination, and you don't get good projects." Eventually, she got very overwhelmed and desperately sought to find her voice and speak out. The environment did not encourage that, and the learning process did not come easily for her. However, Priya eventually sought out and found supportive leaders and coworkers with whom she was able to speak up and receive guidance and encouragement. Once she found the right people to support her and help her get the resources she needed, she was able to speak up against the sexual harassments. Applying the same levels of confidence Priya also learned to say no, and delegate work as needed. "Nobody's gonna tell you, 'Hey, you look tired. Go home.' Nobody's gonna tell you that. They want you to get work done and if it's done nobody pays attention. I had to take care of me."

TOXIC CULTURE, KNOWING WHEN TO MOVE

Marya Kato was born in Minsk, Belarus, and moved to the United States when she was thirteen years old with her mother. In a new country with no money or family, she had to learn to adapt to a new continent, new language, and new culture. She also had to combine menial work with her schooling as a teenager to help support bills. Although she became a citizen at the age of sixteen, there was no college fund and extended family support. It was just herself and her mother.

"I did not have the luxury of anything to fall back on. We came to this country with thirty dollars. So everything that we had, which was not a lot was earned through hard work. I graduated college with a year until I had to start repaying my six-figure college debt." She got her degree in international policy from Hawaii and focused on homeland security. Her first job out of college was with an agency in Washington, DC, tied to both the Department of Homeland Security and the Department of Justice. Since this was in line with where she wanted to be and what changes she desired to make, she happily took the role, excited to put in the work, learn, and grow.

Marya, as a Middle Eastern immigrant, has a slight accent and an obvious Eastern European look. She was constantly subjected to remarks about her looks at work. "I was ready and always willing to work hard and learn. But every time that I would bring my smarts, I would get downgraded only to my looks." Marya had career goals and would always volunteer for tasks and projects. Getting assigned tasks and events were always an opportunity she appreciated until she started getting comments and feedback that the assignments were given due to her looks and not her qualifications.

"I would get sent to events like working field conferences to represent the company and I would always get so excited until once I had the CEO of the company approached me and say, 'You know, we need you to go to this event.' And when I asked why me out of 500 employees that were available to travel, he said, 'Because we need you to be a booth babe.'" Marya was angry and frustrated. Working hard and constantly getting dismissed or recognized for the wrong reasons was discouraging. When you put in long hours and extra learnings, attempting to bring the best to her job, you expect more. However, the attention she got was not what she wanted.

"I was once approached by a board member. And he said, why do you work so hard? You're a good-looking woman. You're young, and you're smart. Why don't you find yourself a rich man?" She eventually realized it was a lost battle and began to look for a different job. Getting the same comments and attitudes from the company leadership and various members of the company made her realize there really was no place to turn. The culture allowed for her colleagues to make these comments without holding them accountable. "The stereotypes and assumptions that were constantly undermining my credibility was taking an emotional toll, and I started to look for another job." Marya was eventually able to get a job at a different company where her work was appreciated, and she could advance.

"Part of what keeps me pushing is because I must. I don't want to be in a situation that my parents were in that brought me here. I don't want to make a situation where I leave my parents, like my mother did hers. I want better for the next generation, for my family, for my children."

Eventually, Marya was able to switch jobs and move to a less toxic environment. She also started an organization that focused on the type of change she wanted to see in the workplace and advance sustainability initiatives. She had to be the champion of her own destiny and learned to ignore the dissenting voices in the wrong environment.

As an immigrant in corporate America, the dream is to have champions and earn respect for your contributions at work. However, it's a journey to get people to see past the stereotypes, which will be different for everyone. Sometimes the effort to try and fit in can be a wasted effort if it is in the wrong environment. Not everyone has the luxury to quit and start a company as Marya did. However, recognizing when the environment is toxic can be a start to developing a plan to exit and look for a different job. There is a health impact when dealing with an environment where blatant bias comes from the top, and the behaviors are allowed to thrive.

Thriving in corporate America can sometimes mean changing jobs—and changing them quickly.

TOXIC BOSSES, KNOWING WHEN TO MOVE

Victoria Wilson grew up in Okinawa, a small island in the middle of the Pacific Ocean. Born to a white mother and an Okinawan father, she grew up surrounded by her father's extended family, and her view of the United States came through the US military. She immigrated to the United States for college. When she got into the workplace after college, she was working off the hierarchical culture that looks up to people in positions of authority as having earned it. "The social contract that I grew up in is that if they're your manager, or if they're in a position of authority, that they were put there because of some merit or some reason." Victoria had obtained two different master's degrees and worked at a few start-ups in marketing and product development. By the time she accepted a contract offer with a big tech company, she knew she was looking to officially move into a people role. "I realized that I really enjoy working with people more than I enjoy selling a product."

At the new company, she had interesting encounters with one of the directors she worked with. The director would yell at his team and get frustrated. "Everybody would very softly work around him and his temper." Once she had a meeting with him, that was set up to be about career development. This was not mandated for contractors, and she was not comfortable having that discussion. However, she was encouraged to participate. In the room, one of the first questions he asked was about her long-term career aspirations. Victoria answered, "Oh, I see myself returning to school to get a doctorate." The director started laughing at what he thought was a hilarious response. He proceeded to explain that he had a doctorate, and it was too hard. "I spent the remainder of the conversation not only trying to justify it, but also downplay the type of degree that I wanted to get, which was an EdD, not a PhD like he had. I was looking at him as kind of like this authority figure, and I internalized that for years. I was thinking, *I'm not worthy; I'm not qualified to do this.* It took so many years to get over the trauma of that experience and get back my confidence."

Victoria successfully completed her doctorate in 2021 from a top-ranked institution. Growing up biracial, she had the cultural experience of observing from the edges and used that to her advantage at work. She was able to assess what toxicity looks like at this big tech company and decided on another career opportunity. As she rightly stated, "Being biracial, we've always been on the periphery. But the great thing about being on the periphery, and even from an immigrant experience, is that sometimes you get to see the whole picture; you get to see the big picture and start making those connections."

THRIVING IN INTERSECTIONALITY IN TOXIC WORK ENVIRONMENTS

Systems are made up of people, and people do not always have the best intentions.

As an immigrant, sometimes it is difficult to recognize toxicity in the workplace. Other times even when recognized, reacting can be difficult or possible options for next steps unclear. The result is a lot of internalized stress that is not healthy. Apart from trying to thrive at work, it is important to recognize that people make up the corporation. It is helpful to know the legal rights and the resources available for support. But certain situations with specific managers, work teams, or organizational culture require switching jobs.

As immigrants, the same background that makes us sensitive to and internalize a lot of aggressive or toxic actions in the workplace also heightens our perceptions. We can recognize individuals and environments that will always hold us back from thriving. It might not always be an immediate option to move, but when the opportunity comes up, it is important to make a change and find spaces that support and embrace our identities and nurture our ambitions.

CHAPTER HIGHLIGHTS

- Know that systems are not perfect, and people are humans.
- Find resources and understand employee rights within your organization.
- Ask questions of the right people, inside or outside the company.
- Understand that not all situations can be resolved by working harder.
- We can't change a culture by ourselves; we all need support.
- Self-advocacy is possible with the right resources.
- Sometimes, the best option is to find a different company.

THE IMMIGRANT IDENTITY DILEMMA IN AMERICA

For immigrants, the journey in corporate America starts with identity.

Filling out demographic data forms in the US always makes me wonder about the options. Do I select "Black/African American" or "Other"? If I chose "Other," how is that interpreted? Where does "Nigerian Born" or "Naturalized American" fit in? Does it really matter? For those who identify as immigrants in America, there are different legal statuses. Some were born in the United States to immigrant parents; some immigrants moved with their families as children, while others, like me, immigrated as an adult. This means that for immigrants in the workplace, we have different types of legal requirements and restrictions. An immigrant in the corporate workplace can be US-born with or without legal restriction, or non-US born with different types of legal restrictions. When it comes to the legal work status in the United States and in the corporate workplace this legal status makes a lot of difference. As we have seen from the experiences of the different women cited in this book, the legal barriers do not only create exclusion during the hiring process but also organizational cultural factors that can also drive exclusion for immigrants within the workplace.

My first full-time job after college was in a global organization at the offices in Lagos, Nigeria. We had many people from other African countries and from different continents. The focus was always to showcase our country in the best possible light. We were vested in making sure they experienced the local culture and knew how to get around, even if the stay was for work. I personally felt a lot of pride when I talked about the local favorite places and treated them to Nigerian cuisine. It did not matter that they were on work visas; they were from other African countries or from Europe. They are not Nigerians, and the goal is to give the gift of a great impression and feel my pride, our pride in our country. Maybe that's where we start with—addressing the individual perspectives in America. Why is that not the feeling that is prevalent in America and in the corporate workplaces? In America, the default is the division that leaves an immigrant struggling to identify where to fit in. The American system wants everyone to fit nicely into certain checked boxes, and these boxes have external boundaries that someone else controls. It starts with acknowledging the division in America as a country that has translated into the corporate workplace.

In America, in the corporate workplace, there is a distinction between "us" and "them." The problem is the multiple definitions of "us" to start with, and the fact that "them" is subjective.

As we start in the corporate workplace in a new country as immigrants, we think, "Who do I need to be in this space?" In America, it might be easier to start with, "Who am I, and how do I represent that here?"

THRIVING IN INTERSECTIONALITY: IMMIGRANTS, BELONGING, AND CORPORATE AMERICA

As immigrants at work, we are on a journey. That journey might start with identity, but that is only the beginning. Depending on the legal aspect, we navigate legal and social learnings to get a job in the corporate workplace—the right career choice, the right organization and role, and even learning the communication style of the organization we work in.

Once we get in, it is important to continue to explore ways to grow. At that intersection of inclusion in corporate America and American immigration law are individuals just like me asking questions about where we fit in. The efforts to be more "American" in the corporate workplace become a process of putting the pieces of America together like a puzzle. Depending on your location, industry, and company culture, the pieces you see look very different, and you don't have a full picture to guide you. Microaggressions and intentional exclusive behaviors can be steeped in unfounded stereotypes about immigrants. One individual cannot control how other people at work behave in the workplace. But as immigrants, embracing the identity helps to move toward discovering the strengths that can be leveraged to thrive in the workplace.

We have been talking about gender equality and equity at work and making slow strides. As we begin to explore different subgroups under the large identity groups at work, we are slowly acknowledging that the intersectionality lens is the broader lens through which we bring everyone together in our differences. As corporate professionals qualified to do the jobs who also happen to be immigrants, it is difficult to fit nicely into any of the existing boxes that a divided country has translated into the workplace, leading to exclusion at work.

Just like every woman I interviewed for this book, the immigrant identity has impacted my career and my life in the last few years. During those first twenty-five years, my world was my family and my local community and network. I didn't think of my place in the global world and did not imagine a world where I am judged simply based on my country of origin and my skin color. That confidence followed me into the United States, where it quickly got eroded by the realities of living and working in corporate America. The process of writing and researching for this book has been a journey to finding that voice back.

Being an immigrant comes with unique perspectives as well as needs and barriers. Until we recognize it as such, we cannot begin to sufficiently support our immigrant colleagues, creating belonging spaces at work that embraces everyone.

As I continue to find my voice, my goal is that this book, these stories, these women, inspire change:
- For the immigrant woman who feels out of place, unseen and unheard in the workplace: You belong, and you deserve to be there as your full self.
- For the leader and diversity, equity, and inclusion professional who is advocating for corporate culture changes, the immigrant dimension and perspective is a unique part to be included.

As we grow, evolve, and get comfortable in embracing our authenticity, we move from the getting in mindset to leveraging our cultural background, not focused on "fitting in" to the corporate organization but on "adding value" in our unique ways.

Although this book strives to maintain a strong positive tone and encourage immigrants on identity and uniqueness, ending with toxic workplaces is also a strong reminder that sometimes spaces will not welcome immigrants. Overall, it is not the responsibility of immigrant employees to help leaders be more inclusive. It is up to everyone at work and especially business leaders and political leaders to create workplaces where everyone can belong. Thriving in intersectionality includes getting the right compensation for our work, getting promoted for a job well done, having access to internal supportive programs to advance our careers in the workplace, and saying yes to not hiding our culture and background at work. This book is to help elevate the right voices, amplify the issues, and build inclusive spaces for immigrants in the corporate workplace so we can continue to accelerate equity and equality in the workplace.

For more resources to support your career journey as an immigrant in the corporate workplace:

Join the LinkedIn group:

"Thriving in Intersectionality—Immigrants in Corporate"

OR

Visit www.immigrantsincorporate.org

ACKNOWLEDGMENTS

———

I am most grateful to God, my good, good Father! You placed gifts, desires, and passions in me and have continually guided me through your word and worship as I continue to take the steps to fulfill my purpose.

To my family, especially my husband, my two sons, and my daughter. Thank you for bearing with me through all the late nights and sometimes grumpy days due to sleeplessness and overwhelm on this journey. All the hours spent moving from an idea to a completed book meant deadlines and more deadlines, hours spent on research, interviews, and editing. To my hardworking and smart sister, my Yetunde Asake Dalley, thank you for all your encouragement, even from a distance. To my dear big cousin Tolulope Martin, who has always been blazing trails for me, praying for and encouraging me as a career mom, a leader, and an immigrant in the corporate world; although on a different continent, we have both made a home away from home, and I appreciate your encouragement.

To my inner circle and board of champions who were always an encouraging text and a phone call away throughout the process of breathing this book into reality while launching a brand new business and running a second business and a home: Damilola Akani, Anne Tosin Musa, Carrie Sawyer, Hauhna Hicks, Anu Iwanefun, Tola Winters. Thank you for never calling me crazy, believing in my dreams, urging me on, praying for and with me, consulting with, and showing up for me, my family, and my visions in your different areas of strength.

I'd like to also thank all the women I interviewed as part of the research for this book. Most were strangers, and not every story made it into the book. However, you all gave insights that shaped the final book and hopefully the beginning of more conversations and ultimately support and changes in the corporate workplace. Thank you for saying yes, trusting me with your stories, and championing me all the way.

Fourth, a huge thank you to the New Degree Press team for all your support. Professor Eric Koester, whose first fifteen-minute call in 2021 gave my "book idea" the very first speck of hope, and the push for a "done first draft" and "shitty first draft." Special shoutout to my developmental editor, Katie Sigler, who started the walk with me and didn't let me give up when it looked impossible to get a first draft done. And to my manuscript revisions editor, Miko Marsh, who walked the last lap with me, cheering me all the way from the shitty first draft to my finished book.

Finally, I want to especially acknowledge everyone who pre-ordered a copy of my book during my pre-launch campaign and spent time as beta readers on my manuscript. Thank you for reminding me that many people truly champion inclusion in the workplace, in America, and beyond.

Supporters and Beta Readers:
Aarohi Thakkar; Adetola Winters; Agatha Asiimwe; Ana Ateca Arevalo; Andrea Gilman; Anne Musa; Annette Fiaty; Anu Adeosun; April Greco; Bethel Fesseha; Betty Huang; Brian Anderson; Carola Nitz; Carrie M Sawyer; Chakravarthi Bokka; Cheli Lange; Cindy Montgenie; Cori Stell; Cristina Bucardo; Dahiana Duarte; Damilola Akani; Damola Adeyemo; David Pryor; Ed Frauenheim; Eric Koester; Gregory Maurie; Idara Ogunsaju; Jennifer Ryan; Jessie Kain; Jill Frack; Jim Young; Jonathan Dumas; Judy Dang; Karin Fair; Kelly Du; Khady Gaye; Leah Draper; Linda Rose-Winters; Madeline Zamoyski; Marc Fields; Martha Burwell; Maureen Booth; Melany del Carpio; Merlin's Kumar; Michael Afolabi Adeyemo; Nat Morgan; Neha Shukla; Nickoria Johnson; Olamide Esan; Olajumoke Kupoluyi; Olanike Ajayi; Olanrewaju Olafisoye; Olariyike Adeyemi; Olayinka Adeyemo; Olumide Aborisade; Osibo Imhoitsike; Ozi Hidalgo Balarezo; Paul Mola; Rajal Ganatra; Rekha Prodduturi; Roger Osorio; Sarah Bacerra; Sarah McGann; Sertrice Grice; Sherri Lynn Kelly; Sherry Hayes; Shevonne Dyer-Phillips; Simone Johnson Smith; Slavica Tomic; Sofia Bonnet; Soliat Adekanye; Stephanie Trevino; Stephen Akinola; Susan Bernstein; Susan Childs; Susan Miller; Susan Oguche; Sylvia DeMott; Temilola Abiola Komolafe; Thomas Foley; Tolu Martin; Victoria Wilson; Wande Shofela.

APPENDIX

INTRODUCTION

`Merriam-Webster. s.v. "intersectionality." Accessed June 19, 2022.
https://www.merriam-webster.com/dictionary/intersectionality.

CHAPTER 1

Ferrera, America. "My Identity is a Superpower — Not an Obstacle."
Filmed April 2019 in Vancouver, BC. TED video, 13:53. Accessed
May 31, 2022.
https://www.ted.com/talks/america_ferrera_my_identity_is_a_
superpower_not_an_obstacle.

CHAPTER 2

Tamir, Christine, and Monica Anderson. "One-in-Ten Black People
Living in the U.S. Are immigrants." Pew Research Center.
February 25, 2022.
https://www.pewresearch.org/race-ethnicity/2022/01/20/one-
in-ten-black-people-living-in-the-u-s-are-immigrants/.

CHAPTER 3

"Directory of Visa Categories." U.S. Department of State.
Accessed May 30, 2022.
https://travel.state.gov/content/travel/en/us-visas/visa-
information-resources/all-visa-categories.html.

"QS World University Rankings 2023: Top Global Universities."
Top Universities. Accessed June 12, 2022.
https://www.topuniversities.com/university-rankings/world-
university-rankings/2023.

Woolston, Chris. "Postdoc Survey Reveals Disenchantment with
Working Life." *Nature News*. November 18, 2020.
https://www.nature.com/articles/d41586-020-03191-7.

CHAPTER 5

"Explore Census Data." U.S. Census Bureau. Accessed May 30, 2022.
https://data.census.gov/cedsci/table?tid=ACSDP5Y2019.DP02.

"The 2021 Global Employee Survey." Globalization Partners.
December 28, 2021.
https://www.globalization-partners.com/blog/2021-global-
employee-survey/.

Made in the USA
Las Vegas, NV
18 October 2022